Robert Henry Cobbold

Pictures of the Chinese, Drawn by Themselves

Robert Henry Cobbold

Pictures of the Chinese, Drawn by Themselves

ISBN/EAN: 9783337166991

Printed in Europe, USA, Canada, Australia, Japan

Cover: Foto ©ninafisch / pixelio.de

More available books at **www.hansebooks.com**

The Chinese at Home.

PICTURES OF THE CHINESE,

DRAWN BY THEMSELVES.

DESCRIBED

BY REV. R. H. COBBOLD, M.A.,

RECTOR OF BROSELEY, SALOP, LATE ARCHDEACON OF NINGPO.

RICE BOWL AND CHOP STICKS

LONDON:

JOHN MURRAY, ALBEMARLE STREET.

1860.

NOTICE.

A RESIDENCE of eight years among the Chinese at the port of Ningpo, with frequent opportunities of travel in the province of Chekeang, enables the writer to offer this unpretending little volume to the English public.

The pen-and-ink etchings, contributed by a native artist, are not the least valuable part of the book. They are faithful representations of the Northern Chinese. The contour of the figures differs much from the prevailing type of the South, and affords a pleasing variety to the hackneyed form to which we have been accustomed.

The only figures of a foreign cast (for all without the boundaries of the province must be accounted foreign) are those of the "fortune-teller" in the sketch "Symbolism of Words;" and of the "phrenologist." Nor is this without reason. Persons who follow such professions are usually strangers. "The prophet without honour in his own country" is a world-wide proverb.

The descriptions which accompany the etchings are mere jottings of what has come under the writer's personal observation; in some instances notes of characters with whom he has been acquainted. Though very imperfect in all but the outline, they may yet give the reader a vivid picture of Chinese habits and customs; just as a simple pen-and-ink etching may prove quite as interesting and accurate as a more elaborate drawing.

BROSELEY RECTORY,
  Nov. 25, 1859.

CONTENTS.

CONTENTS.

捉牙蟲

THE INFALLIBLE REMEDY.

THE CHINESE AT HOME.

No. 1.

THE INFALLIBLE REMEDY.

TOOTHACHE is an universal plague. Every country has a special "nostrum" for its cure. China knows the plague, and China has a nostrum, which may well challenge all others for originality and efficacy. The quacks who in this case advance their specific are all women. I speak of them and their doings as I have seen and known them in the province of Chekeang. Whether they are found elsewhere in China I know not. The remedy they employ has never yet, to my knowledge, been published to the world; and we must not feel surprised if, after this paper has once got abroad, a shipload of these charlatans should be sent for, and make their appearance "one fine morning," in the Thames.

B

These female quacks maintain that the usual
cause of toothache is a little worm or maggot,
which has its nest in the gum under the root, and
if this little offender can be driven or coaxed out,
the gnawing pain will immediately cease. But
how he is to be driven or coaxed out is the secret
of their trade, the knowledge of which they confine
most rigidly to those of their own profession.

We had not been resident many years in the
country before we heard talk of these women and
their wonderful performances, and as my friend
and I took our customary walks together, our conversation not unfrequently turned their way. My
friend stoutly maintained that it was all imposture; it was impossible, he said, that maggots in
the gums or teeth should have escaped the observation of our dentists, who had examined hundreds
of thousands, not merely of teeth, but of mouths
for so many years. "So convinced am I" (he went
on) "of the imposture, that I would not believe it
even were I to see the maggots with my own eyes
crawling forth from the gums." "Come, come," I
said, "I am not such a sceptic as all that; if I
really see a thing, and know there is no collusion,
I believe it; besides, other *great discoveries*" (here
my friend smiled) "have lain hid for ages, and have

quite unexpectedly been brought to light; and still more, how is it that some two thousand of these women find a livelihood in this Ningpo plain? are people such fools as to consult them when they are not suffering? and are they such dolts as to pay their much-loved money for what does them no good?" So we argued on, but our words were as light as the gossamer in their effects; neither of us yielded to the other's arguments. Soon after this we heard that the aid of these women had been called in by foreign residents; one lady especially, who had consulted a surgeon of H.B.M.'s ship ——, and had received no benefit, ready, in her distress, to try any remedy, *fortunately* heard of the fame of these women, engaged one of them to come to her house, and in a few minutes several of the little offenders were safely deposited in a wine-glass; and, what was more remarkable, the tooth-ache ceased for the time to trouble her. Still my friend would not be convinced. Others, again, moved by curiosity, pretended to have the tooth-ache, and these women plied their trade most pro-fitably, drawing, as I was informed, at least twenty of these insects from the mouth of a good-natured captain of a merchant-vessel, whose teeth, from eating hard biscuit all his life, were as sound as a

child's of ten years old. The women quacks were
not in the least disconcerted when they heard that
the gentleman had never been troubled with the
toothache in his life; they obviated this objection
by saying that the teeth, decayed or not, had
maggots in them, and that it was best to extract
them at once for fear of after consequences. In
order that no collusion should be possible, the
precaution was taken of only admitting one woman
at a time, who was previously searched all over by
the mistress of the house. When called upon to
exercise her skill, her arms were bared up to the
elbow, and her hands were always carefully washed
before operating. The same results followed, and
still my friend would not be convinced.

A medical man in the place collected several of
the finest specimens, and preserved them carefully
in spirits of wine, intending to send them shortly
to the United States for inspection. I heard one
of Her Majesty's consuls assert with great vehe-
mence that there could be no imposture in the
matter, he could not possibly be deceived, for he
had seen it with his own eyes. Still my friend
would not give up his point, he would not be
convinced.

One day we were sitting in our rooms, which

were opposite each other, puzzling over the intricate symbols of the native literature, with our respective pundits, or sien sangs, when we heard the well-known cry of these women—" che ngaw gong, che ngaw gong "—I at once called to the servant, " Ask her to come in." We gladly threw aside our books, and both rejoiced at the prospect of an experiment, for we had never yet seen these wonderful practitioners. The first to be operated upon was one of our teachers, suffering from an inflamed *eye;* for the same mischievous little worm causes both the teeth to ache, and the eyes to be inflamed. " This honourable teacher," we began, wishes to consult you ; we will be answerable for the reward of your skill. Look at his eye—do you know what causes that inflammation ?" " Yes, it is a worm." " Can you cure him ?" " I can." The teacher sat down, and the woman, having taken a bright steel pin, about the size of a large knitting needle, from her hair, and having borrowed an ordinary bamboo chopstick from the cook, proceeded to her business. We watched her narrowly. We were indeed much interested in the experiment; chiefly, because we hoped to set at rest our controversy, and also because we had promised her the munificent sum of three-pence per head for all the live stock she captured. She held one of her sticks, the bamboo one, on the corner of the eye, and tapped it lightly with the other, changing occasionally its position. After a few seconds she called our attention with the well-known *naw!* and turning back the eyelid with the steel pin, she took up triumphantly a fat specimen of the tribe, about the size and description of a cheese maggot. This was, I confess, far from satisfactory. I thought to see the little creatures forcing their way out of the flesh; instead of this, the one now shown us lay quietly reposing on the surface of the eye-ball, certainly without motion, if not without life. My friend then said he had many decayed teeth, and wished to know whether he were a subject to exercise her skill upon; she said "decidedly; your teeth are very bad." He sat down, and I watched every motion of the hand and arm; and as one stick held on the tooth was tapped gently with the other, I was reminded of the way in which, as a boy, I used to get my worms for fishing. I found that by simply putting the spade deep in the ground, and by working it quickly backwards and forwards, if there were any worms within a yard of the place, they would all crawl out of their holes and lie on

the surface, and so I obtained them, with a tenth
part of the ordinary trouble and dirt of digging.
Well, before half a minute, the singular sound so
well known in China, "naw!" came again, and
this being twice repeated, my friend was rid of two
intruders. It now came to my turn; the lady was
driving a thriving trade, and an old hollow tooth
was not to be resisted, so my friend now took his
turn to stand and watch, while I submitted to the
bamboo and steel tapping. His eyes were not
better than my own; the "naw" again showed
that prey had been taken. My friend, now almost
in despair, and with that determination which
despair alone, perhaps, imparts, armed himself with
a pocket-handkerchief, and with Argus eye watched
each time that either of the sticks was withdrawn,
and carefully wiped it; he did this so pertina-
ciously, sometimes almost pugnaciously, when the
good lady attempted, after a series of taps, to
introduce the instrument again without being
cleansed, that no more maggots would come out,
and the quack doctress drew herself up and said,
quite authoritatively, "that gentleman has no
more." "Indeed," I said, "I thought to have
given you an opportunity of making a fortune."
We tried in vain to induce her to try her skill on

others of our household. No, she was immovable;
the kerchief was too much for her; she persisted
in saying that our mouths were all perfectly free
from disease, and that we should never have the
toothache again in our lives. But now we had
to pay, according to promise, three-pence per head
for each maggot in the glass; there should have
been four, viz.: teacher with inflamed eye, one;
my friend, two; myself, one; but instead of four,
behold, there were *six* in the cup! As she saw
we were rather angry, she was well content with
her shilling; maintaining, stoutly, however, that
on two occasions a brace had come out together,
which we had not noticed.

Now, strange as it may seem, this was the first
real blow to the practice of these quacks in the
place. We never could induce any of the sister-
hood to come across the threshold of our house
again; and, though they continued to attend other
houses, yet, shortly after this, a bungling old
woman, whose eyesight was getting dim, failed in
her performance, and went away wringing her
hands, and saying, "Ah, stupid, stupid, my poor
old eyes are in fault, they have betrayed me!"

The specimens carefully packed in spirits of
wine did actually leave the shores of China for

the United States; but, fortunately for the credit of the faculty, a letter arrived there before them, which prevented them from occupying the distinguished place intended for them on the shelves of a museum.

No one has ever yet discovered exactly how the trick is done; most of the natives seem to know that it is a trick, but there are still sufficient persons found willing to be deceived, or rather who resort to this remedy and find benefit from it.

Our engraving conveys a very truthful representation of this class of women: they are known by their long umbrellas, their small feet, and their very neat head-dress, and have the character of being well able to defend themselves if rudely attacked. The account goes that one kick with that club foot, and often heavy shoe of theirs, will send a man spinning to the other side of the road. I trust they do not often meet with such treatment as to make them try the experiment.

NINE-STORIED PAGODA.

THE DIVINER.

—

THE DIVINER.

——◆——

IF, as the ancients said, *lucus*, a grove, were so
called "*a non lucendo*," because no light shines
in it, we might suppose that a *seer* was so called,
because in the great majority of cases he saw
nought, and the diviner would have his name
simply because he divineth nothing.

The sapient-looking gentleman, who figures on
the opposite page, is one of the supposed fortune-
tellers in China. Their name is legion, and in
these sketches a few of the more prominent
characters of this class will be introduced.

When the mind of man is not enlightened by
science and revelation, experience teaches us that
it is a prey to various foolish and degrading superstitions. No wonder, then, that in a country like
China, where science has made comparatively so
little progress, and where revelation has scarcely
yet diffused her faintest beams, superstitions of
every kind should be rife. It is a genial climate and a kindly soil, in which they spring up

rank and luxuriant. The workings of natural laws
are at best but partially understood. For example,
the thunder, the fire, the earthquake, the eclipse,
are supposed to be not so much subject to certain
laws, as under the authority and control of some
capricious deity. The ancestor or god of thunder,
luy-tsoo, is worshipped with peculiar honours in
the summer months, when storms are prevalent.
Then crowds of earnest devotees besiege his shrine.
The spirit of fire has innumerable votaries, who
deprecate his wrath in the dry season of autumn.
The earthquake is ascribed to the convulsive
struggles of a huge tortoise to shift the earth
from off his back. The eclipse is said to be caused
by a voracious dog, in his attempts to swallow the
orb of day. And though, with regard to the
eclipse, there are some who know better, and if
they cannot themselves explain the true reason,
know that it has to do with fixed laws, and occurs
at regular periods, noted in the imperial alma-
nacks, yet the same excitement still prevails when-
ever the phenomenon occurs: gongs are beaten,
and crackers are fired from every house to frighten
away the hungry beast. And when the thought
has occurred that through every city, and town,
and village of the eighteen provinces of China

proper, the same gonging and squibbing was at
that very moment going on, the mind could not
forbear the conclusion, that in the popular esteem
superstitious fear must still, when the signs of the
heavens occur, be an uppermost and pervading
feeling.

Nay, even in this enlightened nineteenth century, in the midst of a Christian country, and in
the presence of an open Bible—when the march of
intellect is supposed to have trampled under foot
effete superstitions, as the British soldier has, by
the help of God, trampled under foot the savagery
of sepoy madness—even now witches, wise men,
ugly or pretty gypsies, fortune-tellers of various
grades, are earning a *decent* livelihood amongst us.
Love-sick youths still consult the astrologer to ascertain their hopes of marriage from the stars:
silly servant-girls still make up bundles of clothes
(their own or their mistress's), weighted, if possible, with a piece of plate, a silver spoon or fork,
to obtain dragon's blood, or some other charm,
which is to operate in obtaining for them kind
husbands, a comfortable home, and a sprinkling of
children, as our police reports even for the present
year have shown. And if these things exist
amongst us, with our twenty thousand clergy of

the Established Church, and nearly as many of other denominations, battling more or less vigorously against them; with our mechanics' institutes, our oft-recurring lectures, our libraries and reading-rooms, and generally our educated men of all professions, aiming direct and ponderous blows at their destruction, we must not be surprised if China, with no such privileges and helps, still lies under the potent spell of superstition.

We find it, indeed, to be so, and especially in the particular line of fortune-telling. Man has an intense, and yet insane, desire to pierce into futurity. Having lost the true clue in this labyrinth of life, he seizes every random line which offers a pretence to be a guide in his perplexity. Hence, in China, shops which deal in the knowledge of lucky or unlucky days, which, from the horoscope of your nativity, cast your future lot: stalls, which allure the passenger to stop, that he may learn whether his intended journey or business will be successful, drive a prosperous trade, the keepers of them are clothed in silk and satin, and are often men of apparent refinement and intelligence. Again, you seldom enter a Buddhist temple without seeing some anxious face watching till one of the "sticks of fate" falls out of the

shaken box. This is then picked up and taken to
the attendant priest for interpretation, or, if the
man can read and is satisfied to trust himself so
far in his own hands, he goes to the book wherein
its explanation is written, and gathers from it for
himself, or his parents, his wife, his child, or his
business, what will befall them in the dark future.
These sticks of fate are sixty-four in number, and
they are a vulgar corruption of the sixty-four
diagrams of Fuhhe, which are supposed to contain
an inexhaustible fund of occult wisdom.

But we are letting our figure stand all this time,
and are not paying him that attention which no
doubt he thinks he deserves. He holds in his
hand a short ram's horn, divided longitudinally
into two parts, and, by casting these down before
him, he can judge by their configuration, the
direction in which the point or the base of the
horn turns, either towards any particular quarter,
or towards each other, what your destiny will
probably be. Once, when on my travels, I came
to a road-side temple, where one of these split ram's
horns was kept for the benefit of the traveller.
Many on this occasion were trying their fortune;
some, if they met with what they esteemed rather
a bad-omened configuration, said with great *naïveté*

that they would try again, as it were "appealing from Philip drunk to Philip sober;" some went away with pleased looks, who had obtained at the first throw the hope that their journey or business would be prospered. So I went among them and said, "By your leave, seniors, I will have a throw with the ram's horns." They looked surprised that a foreigner should imitate their customs, for they generally know that we argue against all such superstitious usages. I took the horns, and, with considerable force, *threw them away.* "There," I said, "that is the best throw to make; such things belong to *seay kęaou*—corrupt religions. You ought to have nothing to do with them. Don't your own books tell you that the fear of Heaven's law (*Hwuy Teen ming*) is the first great principle? Do what is right—trust to the guidance of Heaven —and you will be far removed above all such non-sensical observances." They were not angry; indeed, they take in good part all such exhortations, and usually end with, "Your words are right; what you say is quite true." I said they ended here; but no, I wish they had. They ended by going and picking up the split ram's horn, and putting it again in its place; and so I moved on, and the folly that I left behind me still lived to mock me. Follies and vices do live to mock earnest men, and sadden their hearts; but they shall not always live: they were born in time, and they shall die in time. Truth alone existed before the worlds, and shall live after them. In the words of no mean writer, "Great is the truth, and mighty above all things; it endureth, and is always strong—it liveth, and conquereth for evermore; she is the strength, kingdom, power, and majesty of all ages. Blessed be the God of truth."

CHINESE JUGGLERS.

ICE HOUSES NEAR NINGPO.

打花鼓

STREET SINGERS.

STREET SINGERS.

THE original heading of this picture, as given by my Chinese artist, is "striking the flower drum." For the information of those who do not understand the Chinese idiom we must say that flower or flowery (for the position of the word alone determines its genus) is put for anything gay, and frequently means that which is not only gay and pleasing to the eye or senses, but sometimes also that which is dissolute and vicious. Thus "a flower boat" is a boat for a party of pleasure, used frequently by the Southern Chinese for an occasion of revelling and vice. A flower chair is the sedan chair used on occasions of a marriage festivity; flower guns are guns for purposes of amusement, namely, squibs, rockets, and fireworks generally. The meaning of "a flower child" would never be guessed by the English reader; it signifies nothing more than a beggar, most probably because beggars are usually a vagabond people, leading a wretched abandoned life. The Chinese beggar, like his

European brother, notwithstanding all his hardships, greatly prefers his liberty with an occasional feast, frolic, and dance, to the toil of honest industry. I have myself in China clothed, fed, and housed a starving beggar boy, who ran away from me directly he was asked to take a spade and dig for an hour in the garden.

The women in our picture are a kind of beggars, and as they play sprightly, exciting music, and sing gay and almost indecent songs, and I fear live frequently a corrupt life, they are called those who "strike the flower drum." The drum is not the only instrument they employ, but this is put generally for all other kinds of music. One of the figures is seen holding a small drum and a little slip of bamboo as drum-stick, the other has a tiny brass gong, and as she strikes her "flower gong," she deadens the sound with the other hand, to prevent the prolonged clang of the metal from drowning the words of her song. The little child carried on the back shows the ordinary method employed by beggars of stowing away their children when they are too young or too tired to follow their elders on foot.

These street singers are not seen all the year round, they only appear on New-year festivities, when more licence is allowed. Generally there is great decorum in the public streets, the eye is never pained with those painted and bedizened figures which nightly throng our thoroughfares. Our artist has not failed to exhibit with great accuracy the head-dress and general costume of the Chinese women. They vary much in different localities. In the northern provinces, with which I am most familiar, the woman, from some unknown cause either of diet, climate, or mode of tonsure, invariably becomes bald on the front and top of her head by the age of thirty years. This deficiency would seriously interfere with her good looks, and spoil the little beauty she possessed, were it not compensated by a large ornament of false hair, which spreads out from the back of her head like a butterfly's wings.

Women of the class represented in our picture affect long nails, which are a recognized sign of refinement. We are now so familiar with the large embroidered sleeves, the loose jacket, the rich skirt, and the lace-fringed trowsers of the native women, that these features of their costume need no description. Beneath the last peep out the little feet (*how* little only actual observation will make us believe), which are the mark of birth, breeding, and elegance. A foolish fashion, and nothing else, determines the shape and size of the foot, and as half a century ago the smallest waist was the boast of the rival beauties in the English ball-room, and the theme of admiring gallants, so now among the Chinese the tiny foot is of itself a sufficient index of elegance of life; it is of more importance in the eyes of a suitor than a pretty face, and is everywhere the particular vanity of gay society. Our street singers have not neglected to employ this as one enhancement of their personal charms. But we will leave these beggars, for such they are, and vicious beggars too, to sing their New-year's song, and to earn their New-year's fee, wishing them only for the future a better and more honourable occupation.

MANDARIN IN A SEDAN-CHAIR.

賣
飾

No. 4.

THE BARLEY-SUGAR STALL.

THIS will be a tempting paper for children, who
may like to hear something of comfits, barley-
sugar, and sweetmeats on the other side of the
globe.

A sweet tooth seems to be Nature's commonest
gift; for where is the child that does not gaze, with
watering mouth, on the gay lozenge-bottles in the
confectioner's window, and whose little hands do
not clap for joy when Everton toffee is in process of boiling in the pot, or hard-bake simmering
in the oven? I have often noticed longing eyes
watching the pan of boiling sugar at the corner of
some thoroughfare, or under the porch of some
well-frequented temple in China; and as the desired
consistency was attained, the sugar-stick drawn
out to the proper thickness, the elegant spiral
twist given by a dexterous movement of the hand,
and as the long scissors snipped the transparent
and fast-hardening stick into convenient inches, I
have seen the young urchins who were fortunate

enough to possess a few cash, come forward and
eagerly seize the treasure. Not having graduated
as a sugar-boiler, or comfit-maker, I cannot describe, as I should wish to do, the many processes
by which the various tempting sticks or cakes are
manufactured. I shall only say that I have always
much admired the talent, which out of a little
sugar, a few walnuts or almonds, a little grated
ginger or other spice, could bring forth such
variety, both of shape and colour, and such pleasing taste to the palate. Certain I am of this,
that if one of these confectioners could only make
his way with his stall and cooking apparatus to
the corner of Regent Street or Pall Mall, he would
not have to struggle on wrestling with poverty,
but would soon be able to return to his native land
with a fair competency for life. You notice that
the figure in our sketch has two baskets, or rather
tubs, the one containing his goods in the form of
sweetmeats of various devices, the other the fire-
pans and implements necessary for their manufacture. When he moves from place to place, that
short pole which is resting by his side is laid upon
his shoulder, and a tub hangs on a hook at either
end. Listen! He is striking with a flat piece of
brass his little sounding gong, which, with its

clang, clang, clang, invites customers. Each trade
has its own particular cry or call, some vocal, some,
as in this case, instrumental. See! an urchin, whose
fingers are evidently so burnt with the money that
they can hold it no longer, is running forward to
make a purchase. You may tell he is very young,
for his tail is not yet grown, his head is entirely
shaved, save two little tufts of hair, which are
twisted and bound up into a soft horn, and ornamented with a piece of crimson silk. Though so
young, yet he has his own mind about his money,
and very likely will prefer giving that funny-look-
ing wheel in front of the sweetmeats a turn, to
know whether he is to have double the worth of
his money in sugar, or none at all. The gambling
spirit is even strong in infancy, and though the
chances are that the sweetmeat-seller will gain,
yet he cannot resist the temptation; only think, if
he should get two pieces of sugar instead of one!
If he loses, he will stand there watching while
others take their turn; if he wins, he will run
home delighted with his success. Children are
children all the world over, they will have their
fun and frolic, the sweet tooth can never be pulled
out; if it could, what would become of the poor
lollipop-makers!

CHINESE VASE
ENAMELLED WITH ANIMALS.

THE PHYSICIAN.

—

THE PHYSICIAN.

———

IT was quaintly observed to me the other day, that for the practice of medicine you "did not want to know what was inside a man." The meaning of which simply is, that symptoms of disease are of more importance to be known than the disease itself. For the sake of Chinese practitioners, I trust that this saying is true, for they certainly do not "know what is inside a man," nor have they any correct notion where the different internal organs are situated. That which always amuses our exact anatomists is the *scheme* (for I can call it nothing else) of the human frame in Chinese drawings. The heart of man is where every one thinks it ought to be, in the centre, and the other organs range themselves round it, like ministers of state attending on their sovereign. There is an even balance of power, resulting from the idea of order, which holds so prominent a place in every Chinese mind. But it is not as surgeons

and anatomists, but as physicians that we have
now to do with them.

Healing is with them most decidedly a *science;*
they have indeed their quacks as we have, but the
regular practitioner is one who treats diseases
according to certain rules, and who never puts
patients to torture or to death, save strictly *selon
la règle.* I fear that I shall convey to the reader
but a poor idea of the native physician's art, and
that my talented native friend, who gives me such
telling pictures, will find this one but feebly illustrated by my remarks. The fact is, that the
Chinese practice of medicine is not easy for a
foreigner to understand; for the system on which
they found their modes of cure has no parallel
with that of our own country. I must, however,
make an attempt, and if I fail, my friend the artist
must try and wield the pen with as good effect as
he has wielded the brush.

In the fourth moon a great stir is visible in all
Chinese cities. You are constantly meeting with
men clad in brick-red garments, with manacles on
their hands; children sometimes appear attired in
the same strange fashion; on inquiry, we learn
that this is the ordinary prison-dress, and these
men call themselves, and teach the children to call

themselves "culprits." Gangs of them may be sometimes seen passing rapidly through the streets, wildly dangling their hand-cuffs and chains. On further inquiry, we learn that these, young and old, are persons who have been visited with some sore sickness during the previous year, and they come in this humble "culprit" guise to return their thanks to the deities who have helped forward their cure. These deities are about to be honoured with one of the grandest feasts held during the whole year. Thousands of pounds are annually expended to do them service. I cannot now describe the extent and magnificence of this pageant, which distinguishes the fourth month of the year from all other months. I may only just say that each of the five deities has a retinue, which would be no mean appendage to a sovereign's triumphant march; and that the beast of good omen, the dragon, figures in the rear of each compartment of the five-fold procession. What I want to tell the reader is, that these five deities are the gods of the five elements, and that their power to heal diseases depends upon the *fact*, that man's constitution is composed of these five elements, mixed up in him in different proportions, so that if all remain in harmony he is in health;

if any one predominate so as to have undue ascendancy, his system is deranged, and he suffers. The five elements over which these deities preside are King, Muh, Shwuy, Ho, Too, which five words mean respectively Gold (or metal), Wood, Water, Fire, and Earth. Now I think the reader will agree that, in order to understand a system like this, we have to get rid of many preconceived opinions, and he will not expect me therefore to give a very full, lucid, or satisfactory account of its working.

It is, however, intimately connected with our physician, who, in any derangement of stomach, has to ascertain which of the five elements is preponderating, and then to counteract its influence by proper antidotes. I may throw a little light on the subject by stating that a native friend of mine used to be very much concerned to see me eating so much roast meat, till he observed also another habit, which set his mind at rest about me. He thus expressed himself: "Senior, I used to be distressed when I saw you eat so much roast meat, but now I see why it does not injure you; you drink large draughts of cold water, so that the fire is put out!"

This is the orthodox system of medical treatment; and a foreign physician, who does not adopt a little of their phraseology, has but small chance of success in gaining and keeping patients.

It matters, in fact, little whether you say a man has fever, and you will give him a fever powder, or that the element of fire predominates, and you must give him wood or water, as the case may be, for (as I confessed above) I do not understand the intricacies of the system. "The proof of the pudding is in the eating," is a proverb which will apply to medicine as well as to cookery.

It is true we hear of strange remedies, such as stags pounded and made into pills, which, if the horns were included, I should consider a weak decoction of hartshorn; and who knows but the bones may have similar virtue to the horns; yet such as these are, after all, only quack medicines, and do not belong strictly to the profession.

I have myself no mean idea of Chinese medical skill. It would not be safe to compare it with the advanced state of the science among western nations, but their doctors are decidedly skilful, and, what is more, successful in their treatment of many complaints.

We had a youth in our employ whom we sent down to Hong-Kong for his education at the college, and he was returned to us with a letter, saying that he could not possibly live three months, that climate had nothing to do with the complaint, but that he had been sent back that he might die among his own friends. This was the opinion of two European medical men, who had been consulted for him by those under whose care he was placed. A quaint old doctor, quite a character in his way, took him in hand; his prescriptions were to be checked, if necessary, by one of ourselves. After a short time, he began slowly to recover, and the native physician had the impudence to say that if one item of his prescription had not been omitted, he would have been by that time perfectly restored. I must confess to the crime of having consulted occasionally a native practitioner, and, as it is a rule with me not to seek advice without the intention, at least, of following it, I most conscientiously allowed the prescription he gave me—not the piece of red paper, gentle readers, on which it was written, that were an easy matter,—but the "150 pills twice a day," which the chemist made up to order. A dose of Chinese medicine is quite a curiosity, it is about the size of half a pound of moist sugar, and consists of twenty separate little packets, four or five kinds of bark, a little orange-peel, some walnuts, some gentian and half a dozen other roots, a black treacly mass, not unlike a small cake of blacking; these are all boiled together, and a good half-pint of the decoction is to be taken, *quite hot.* What would the "small dose" and the "single dose" of Homœopathy say to this? The Chinese physician confines himself entirely to his calling; he examines the diagnosis of the disease, writes you out a prescription, which you take to your own chemist to be made up. The lowest fee for a visit is 60 cash, or about two pence; and the coolies of the sedan have also to be paid. The fee advances by 60 cash at a time, so that 60, 120, 180, 240, &c., are the rates, according to celebrity; *very* seldom, however, is a single visit charged more than 180 cash, or sixpence.

When you consult a physician, his mode of proceeding is this: he lays your hand on a soft cushion, feels your pulse at *both* wrists, asks your age, and the symptoms of your indisposition, looks you attentively in the face, sapiently strokes his moustache, and then writes out with that paper and ink, which you see by our engraving is ready prepared, the prescription which you are to follow. Many of these physicians have great celebrity in the treatment of certain diseases; they have possession of family secrets which have been handed down for many generations.

No previous examination is required to qualify for practice. The field is entirely open. It is thought that no restrictions are necessary, but that people may be safely left to their own choice of a physician; and if they suffer, it is their own fault, and they must blame themselves. Sometimes a compact is made to cure for so much money; in case of failure, nothing is to be given beyond the mere price of the medicine taken; but this belongs rather to the quack than to the regular practitioner. I have known a case of mental derangement (which our doctors could not touch) undertaken on these terms, which proved eminently successful. The sum of five dollars only was asked, two of which were deposited for cost of medicine, and the other three were to be given on the patient's recovery. Cases bordering on the ludicrous have not unfrequently happened, where the hard-hearted physician and the eager parents or friends of the patient have been heard bargaining by the hour together about the sum to be paid for the cure.

Our quacks have much yet to learn; a visit to such a country as China would do them good.

和
尚

THE BUDDHIST PRIEST.

—

THE BUDDHIST PRIEST.

—◆—

THE bare-legged, bare-footed figure in our sketch has travelled many a weary league in carrying on his work. His province is to beg—not for himself, but for the monastery to which he belongs. Every large establishment of this kind has priests of different ranks and different occupations. Supreme over all is the abbot, or superior, who has his own private apartments, dines, except on great occasions, at his own table, and enjoys a comfortable income. His duty is to entertain distinguished visitors of the monastery, to administer its revenues, to watch over the due performance of the services of the sanctuary, and to regulate and enforce its discipline in the priests committed to his authority. In the execution of his duties, he has the benefit of an assistant, as sub-prior, who also has his own private apartments, and who attends to minor matters of detail. Subordinate to the abbot and his assistant are the ordinary priests, the greater part of whom employ their time in lounging about; some, studiously inclined, frequent the library, and pore over its voluminous contents; some are engaged in cultivating the fields and tending the forests with which the monastery has been endowed; some, again, are the cooks of the establishment, and display no mean skill in the preparation of their vegetable cuisine; others, either singly or in pairs, start forth from time to time on a begging expedition, when money is needed for the repair of the buildings, or when an unusual influx of priests or unpropitious seasons have made the inmates feel the pangs of hunger; and all, in rotation, take part in the frequent and regular chaunted services before the colossal figures in the central hall.

Buddhism in China is not what it once was in power and influence. The monasteries which we now see were the creation of an age which believed in this religion; some of them are the monuments of imperial zeal. But this faith seems now to be gradually dying out; its sacred edifices are falling into decay, and no new temples are rising. The priests are generally uneducated men, and held in great contempt by the gentry. Imperial patronage, too, is wanting; the present sovereign of the country is either unable or unwilling to raise and endow new foundations, or even to restore and maintain those which his forefathers erected.

In the many monasteries which I visited, I can call to mind but few which indicated, by the care bestowed on them and the strict observance of the rules, that there was reality in the members, or which contained men of superior intelligence. Priests of earnest mind will often heave a deep sigh over the degeneracy of the present age.

In Buddhism there is no distinct order of "begging friars," but, as need arises, a few are chosen to travel through the country and collect subscriptions. In their journeys they are received and lodged by the brethren in other monasteries, who, by a law of the order, are bound to extend to them for a stated time such hospitality. They visit alike the houses of the rich and of the poor, and usually bring the artillery of their arguments to bear upon the weaker sex.

A wallet at their back receives the contributions of the charitable—generally in the form of a little cooked rice, all animal food being prohibited according to the terms of their religious vow. They are the most strict vegetarians in the world, and have not the art of drawing the subtle distinctions between meats discovered by some religionists, or of discovering the essential difference between beef, mutton, and poultry, and salt, butter, eggs, and fish. A piece of common cake, if it contain a particle of either lard, butter, eggs, or milk, is most heretical food; a piece of cheese would be an unpermitted delicacy; a glass of any fermented liquor, a gross violation of propriety. Even the onion is disallowed as too stimulating; the milder and more innocent leek must flavour their porridge.

The priest, as he journeys, gives notice of his approach by striking his *muh-yu*, which is fastened round his waist, as represented by our artist. This curious instrument is also used in the temples as an accompaniment to the prayers, and no one can ever forget the peculiar hollow sound of tapping which issues from the Buddhist monasteries. Some persons are moved by pity to bestow a little rice, or a few copper coins, on a poor old man; others see in him far more than a mere famished beggar, and remember that " he who helps a priest forward on his way, or contributes to the support of a monastery, performs a meritorious deed, which will tend to advance him in the next world."

The mendicant friar is generally chosen for this function from his superior "sanctity;" that is, because he has devoted himself in a marked way to the duties of his monastic life, and is able, through personal conviction of their value, to recommend the prayers and austerities of his system. He will frequently leave with any whom he finds more susceptible of religious impression, some charm, some little scraps of yellow paper, which are thought to be influential in the unseen world, furnishing a viaticum for the fortunate possessor; he will sell a string of holy beads, or leave behind a manual of devotion.

The priests of Buddha, with the exception of a few filthy devotees, have all the head shaved, wear a loose yellow robe and very large stockings, the sign (they say) of an easy temper. Some of the more austere practise self-torture; their shaven head is seen disfigured by the marks of burning, or their hand has lost one or more of the fingers, which have been charred to the stump. This mutilation is very abhorrent to Chinese feeling; "not to deface the body which our parents have bequeathed to us," is a primary maxim of filial duty. The infliction of such mutilations is not, however, always attended with the degree of pain which might be expected. I remember to have seen a priest with two fingers which had been burnt down to the second joint in the flame of a candle, and on

my looking horrified, and expressing my surprise
that he could have endured so much agony, "Oh!"
he said, "it was hardly any pain at all: I first tied
the finger so as thoroughly to numb the extremity,
and then gradually burnt it away." Here is genuine
Chinese character. This man would have credit
for superior sanctity, without going through the
fiery ordeal necessary to that sanctity. "What a
degenerate worm," methinks I hear some Hindoo
fakir say; "I glory in my agony, it makes atone-
ment for my sin."

How remarkable a difference is there in the
power of that wondrous faculty of the mind—
conscience! The poor Hindoo devotee is distracted,
agonized by the sense of sin: the calm, cold-blooded,
worldly Chinese is able to cover all over with the
salve of self-complacent propriety. Which of these
two types of character will prove the more genial
and receptive soil for the seed of Christian truth
events only can disclose. The luxury of saving
one's self is not readily foregone; proud man does
not like to be so indebted to a Divine Benefactor.
But, on the other hand, which spiritual battery
shall make any impression on this sand-bank of
the sensual Chinese mind? Who shall effectually
teach the death-cold secularist the higher interests

of life, and persuade him earnestly to pursue them?
Buddhism has tried, but has failed in retaining its
hold on the popular mind. Its monasteries are
crumbling away, its priests are illiterate and poor,
its religious influence is waning; over the women
of the country only, and the aged in their dotage,
does it retain any power. The human mind, as it
awakes from its lethargy, can never be satisfied
with the fables of the Buddhist priests, with their
anti-social system, their irrational teaching of the
transmigration of souls, and ultimate absorption
into nonentity. Buddhism has, indeed, succeeded
in awakening the conscience, in inspiring hopes
and fears of another state, and in so far may have
paved the way for the introduction of Christian
truth; but it has not been able to furnish the great
example of a man alive to all the instincts of
humanity, nor to declare the higher and essential
truths of spiritual religion. We may therefore be
allowed to express our hope and belief that the day
is not far distant, when the great facts of Revelation shall exert their power over the millions,
now ignorantly and vainly seeking for rest in
Buddhist superstitions.

MENDICANT PRIEST OF BUDDHA.

假髮兒針

—

THE COLLECTOR OF REFUSE HAIR.

—◆—

TO what strange shifts and expedients are many driven by the hard pressures of life to earn the means of barely supporting existence! Any one, who is acquainted with the lower phases of London life, is well aware that thousands scrape together a living out of the dust-heaps in Paddington. Some in rags, some in bones, some in street manure, some in scraps of tin and iron, find support for themselves and their families.

Man is not responsible for his natural powers, nor is it any disgrace to be so deficient in intellect as to be obliged to follow a mean employment. No toil debases man save that which injures his moral character.

Our picture presents to our notice one of the meanest of Chinese callings; and in the refuse hair-gatherer, our artist has not failed to give you a specimen of humanity in one of its lowest forms. But even such a case as this is not without its interest. From the maker of wigs, false beards, and

moustache, and from the worker in ornamental hair
generally, such a calling may justly attract observation. Without the aid of the poor hair-gatherer,
how should that fashionable young man, who, Absolom like, prides himself upon his hair, and yet
unlike Absolom has but little of his own to boast
of, appear in proper guise before his compeers in
society? How, again, shall the coy maiden find,
unless by the same help, those magnificent "butterflies' wings"* of glossy hair, which ornament the
back of her head? But I have unwittingly anticipated: by this time the reader surmises the functions of our friend going his wearisome rounds
with his light wicker-basket. He is either buying
or begging all the refuse combings of the women's
long black hair, which others, skilful in their art,

* The "butterflies' wings" are the highest ornament in hair with
which the Chinese are acquainted. They are always worn by the
women to increase the apparent bulk of hair. A little sketch of
them, drawn from life, may be of more interest to the reader than
any mere description.

CHINESE WOMAN'S HEAD-DRESS, SHOWING THE "BUTTERFLIES' WINGS."

make up into tails, either to supply a need which unfortunately may have arisen, or to increase the proportions of that which nature had too sparely bestowed. As you pass down a Chinese street, you will occasionally see a shop where were sold long switchy horse-tails; such, at least, they long appeared to the writer of these sketches; inquiry at last dissipated the delusion; appearances answered to their proverbial deceitfulness, and these long-switch tails were formed of the refuse combings collected by our persevering friend, and hung in the shop ready to be braided into the usual queue worn by the men.

My mistake as to the true character of these queues is less strange than it may at first appear; the hair of both Chinese men and women not differing very perceptibly from horse-hair. In fact, the hair of the Chinese people is singularly coarse, arising partly from the custom of shaving the head immediately after birth, and continuing to do so at intervals for two years. I am sure that if a single hair were pulled from the head of a Chinese, and from a black pony's long tail, very little difference between the two would be found.

These are the only purposes, to my knowledge,

to which these sweepings of hair are put. No sentimental youth wears a watch-guard made of the loved one's hair; no parent wears the ring or brooch, enclosing the glossy lock of the much-loved child; no gentle sister's arm is encircled with the bracelet, woven with the hair from the fair head, now laid low in the dust; to Chinese hearts all such refinements are unknown; for refinement and delicacy of feeling are the products of Christian civilization, which has not yet shone on the land of the children of Han.

It may surprise the reader, especially if he be a barber or hair-dresser, that I have said nothing about wigs, false beards, and moustache. The fact is, that wig-making is another refinement of which the Chinese know nothing. If there be ever so small a portion of hair on which to attach a tail—it may be only the "grey hafflets" of old age—this necessary appendage is affixed; but if nature has deprived altogether of hair, the head remains in unsightly baldness. Beards also, and moustache, are only used in the mask of the play-actor, and have but little art expended on their construction. We do not, therefore, find merchants travelling through the provinces of China, as they do through those of France and Germany, for the purchase of heads of hair from the peasantry. A simple queue of braided hair is a widely-different affair from our fashionable wigs. The colour is universal, the very name by which the people call themselves is "the race of the dark-hair" (*le ming*), and, save in length and thickness, one Chinaman's queue is very much like another.

CHINESE GENTLEMAN AND SERVANT.

PILGRIM-SHAPED BOTTLE,
ENAMELLED WITH BUTTERFLIES.

收字紙

THE COLLECTOR OF PAPER SCRAPS.

WE are here introduced to a subject of much interest, though it may not altogether engage our sympathy. All have heard of the great respect paid by the Chinese to learning. This respect is even extended to scraps of printed or written paper. In nothing is the peculiarity of this strange people more conspicuous than in this : while we freely use up for any purpose all refuse paper, the Chinese most diligently guard it from abuse. It is not, as is sometimes argued, that they reverence scraps of old paper so as to idolize *them*, but that they venerate so highly the gift of a written language as not to endure that a single word of it should be profaned. No act of foreigners exposes them to such severe criticism and even censure, as their carelessness about the use of paper covered with writing. How (it is asked) can you endure to see a piece of paper lying in the dirt, which may have on it the very name of the Supreme Being? I well remem-

E

ber that there was on one occasion a serious stir among the members of the native churches, and the question was raised, whether they should not unitedly address foreign missionaries on the subject of their improper use of printed books. There were other of our customs sufficiently repulsive to them, but with these they could bear; the profaning of printed paper, however, was a barbarism which even they, the Christian natives, thought should be resisted. It is very difficult for us to realize the intense feeling which this matter has excited; and if ever there was a case where the apostle's rule not to eat that which offended his brother applied, it would be this. No one denies that their feeling is a right feeling, though we may justly think that it is carried to excess. The possession of a literature seems to be that one gift which most of all distinguishes man from the other animals. Natural appetites, speech, and, to a certain extent, reason, or its counterpart, instinct, they have in common with us; but the power of recording past acts, of giving permanency to the thoughts, of conveying, by the mere arbitrary stroke of a pen, very difficult and complex ideas, seems most of all to distinguish man from the brute creation.

Some of the native Christians have tried to frame

excuses for the abuse of our own paper. They have said, words do not necessarily mean to foreigners what they mean to us; for example, "man" with the foreigners is nothing but the three letters m, a, n, and these letters mean nothing till they are put into a sentence, and made to have a connection with other words; while with us the word man is a symbol which, wherever we see it, expresses at once to the eye and mind the idea of a human being. Such excuses are well meant; but they will not reach our case. If we are in fault, this will be found but poor salve with which to heal the sore. This may appear a frivolous matter to us, but it is really a very serious one in China; and it will not do to regard with contempt prejudices so strong as this. I believe that our reputation for civilization and refinement has suffered more from this cause than any other. It is not thought possible that we can have anything worthy the name of a language or a literature, if we permit books, or portions of them, to be trodden under foot, or if we wrap up dirty parcels with printed paper, or even wipe off with it ink or dirt from the table. Every scholar keeps in his study a waste-paper basket, which is accurately represented in the hand of the figure standing at the door of his house; this,

when in use, is hung against the wall, and receives
from time to time the scraps which have been
scribbled upon, or any, even the smallest, piece of
waste-paper which contains only half a letter of
writing.   When the cry of the man with the large
baskets, *King sih sze tsze*, " Revere and spare the
printed paper" is heard, then he will go or send
his servant to the door, and empty the contents of
his basket into the light and capacious skep of the
collector.   This collector is usually employed by a
company of scholars; as in this case the letters on
his little flag inform us that he belongs to the
" great literary society."   The paper thus collected
is burnt in a separate fire-place, often erected in the
side court (the kitchen stove is too profane a place)
of a temple; and by the more strict scholars even
the ashes are not allowed to become the sport of
the four winds, but are taken to some tidal or
running stream and emptied into the waters.   In
the city of Ningpo, distant only fifteen miles from
the sea, I have known them put in charge of a
trusty servant, floated down to the mouth of the
river, and then cast into the strong ebb tide, that
they might mingle with the waters of the wide
ocean, and be effectually saved from all fear of pro-
fanation.

挑

酒

THE WINE-CARRIER.

THE WINE-CARRIER.

CHINA will be peculiar: while she makes as much fermented liquor as any nation, she knows neither beer from malt, nor wine from grapes. If her poets praise her wines, instead of the luxuriant, purple-clustered vine, the dull, prosaic *no-me* rice must be their theme. A considerable breadth of land in the vicinity of all large cities is sown with this particular grain. The blade is of a rich dark green, which distinguishes it from the common rice, and it is harvested somewhat later than the ordinary crops. This rice, when prepared, is remarkably large, soft, and white. Besides its use for wine, the grain, boiled and pounded, is made into white cakes, which are moulded by the hand into every imaginable device, and slightly touched, where necessary, with vermillion or other rich colouring.

China is emphatically a sober country: though her wine is cheap, sound, and good, though there

is no tax upon it, and no restriction whatever in
its sale or manufacture, though nearly all persons,
both men and women of all classes, freely use it,
but few comparatively drink to excess. A drunkard reeling through the streets—which is a very
common disfigurement of life in our cities—is a
rare sight, even in her great seaport towns. During
a residence of many years, at one of these seaports,
I can only call to mind a very few instances of
intoxication.

This wine or spirit—for the word (*tsiew*) means
any fermented liquor—is of two kinds, one made
by the simple process of fermentation, called the
laou tsiew, or old wine, the other a spirit distilled
from this called *seaou-tsiew*, or by our soldiers and
sailors at Canton *samshoo*. The former is drunk
at every meal. The distinction which obtains
among ourselves, of breakfast, dinner, and tea, is
not found in China, nor is it the habit of her
people to sip tea, coffee, or chocolate with their
meals. The only beverage taken with the meal is
this *no-me* wine ; tea is used before or after, but
is never brought on the table at meal-time. The
wine is served up hot, in metal pots like a small
cocoa-pot, is poured into chinaware cups, and a
constant supply of the heated wine comes in, as it

is needed, from the culinary regions. The guests sit at square tables, whose proper complement is four persons, though at crowded entertainments six, and even eight, can find room. The master, at his own table, pours out the first cup of wine for his guests, and when all are filled, each raises his own cup, inclines his head forward, and bows to the others, and sometimes touches his cup with the host's in old-fashioned English style. At the other tables there is usually a strife who shall perform this office. The youngest almost always prevails; and the duty, by common consent, devolves upon him. There is no religious ceremony observed— no libation to the gods—as in the feasts of the ancient Romans.

Though, as we have said, the Chinese are not addicted to drunkenness, yet they consider it a great mark of excellence to have a large power of drinking wine. This they call the *tsiew leang*, or wine-capacity; and it is a common compliment to tell a man that his "wine-capacity" is great, and to urge him to swallow large potations. A story is current among them of a great wine-drinker, who was able to sit on all the day at table, and after consuming what would have been sufficient to drive the reason out of half-a-dozen men, would rise up perfectly sober. The Emperor, hearing the fame of this deep drinker, asked him to dinner, that he might test his marvellous powers. As the story goes, the king had ordered a hollow figure to be cast in bronze, of the exact size and model of this man, and as the wine was served, for each cup that the guest drank, a similar cup was poured into the opening on the top of the head of the image. This went on for some hours, until at length the bronze statue *overflowed*, while the guest continued at the table and rose from it perfectly sober!

The Chinese have the idea—which is found also elsewhere—that persons of great talent are frequently gifted with very strong heads—that such as Johnson or Pitt could never really be made drunk; potations which would drown weaker minds in inebriety, having, as they think, no effect but to elevate the spirits of powerful minds. The jars which contain the wine, and in which it is sold by the manufacturers, are represented in the picture. They are slung in a slight wicker-work frame, and are carried by a short pole over the shoulder. The earthenware of which they are formed is of a coarse kind, and the jar is fastened at the top with hardened clay; a seal is then stamped at the surface, which gives the brand both of the vintage and the manufacturer.

The distilled spirit, or *samshoo*, is never heated; nor is it drunk with the ordinary meals, but is brought on the table in hot weather, and served with biscuits, or some slight repast in the middle of the day.

The common wine is not unlike a dry Sherry or Cape, and is a pleasant bitter, provocative of appetite. It will not bear the admixture of water, and needs no preparation, save heating over a clear charcoal fire. Either from peculiarity of soil which affects the quality of the grain, or from the difference of water, or superior skill in the manu-facture, some places very far excel others in their reputation for good wine. That of Shaou-hing, a few miles south of Hang-chow, is the most noted in the north-eastern provinces. This wine is much approved by the people generally; nor even to the European palate is it distasteful, when use has somewhat habituated us to the flavour. Some of our most admired wines are hardly palatable to the uninitiated: use only familiarizes us to the flavour, and an acquired taste leads us to praise them. The ancients used to flavour their wines with salt water, and impregnate them with pitch, resin, turpentine, and other aromatic ingredients, after which they placed them in the *fumarium*, or smoke-kiln, to ripen them, and impart to them a smoky flavour. This practice is in part followed by the modern Greeks, which makes their wines most unpalatable to all but the natives. Nor are we altogether clear of the charge of a vitiated palate—much of the peat-smoked whiskey is made up to suit the depraved taste of the southerner.

Wines made of fruits, especially of the peach, are occasionally found at the tables of the rich. Sometimes, by private individuals, a kind of noyeau is made by steeping the sliced rind of the pommelo fruit in the strong spirit, and then softening its rough flavour with sugar; but in a hundred feasts, taken at random, no other wine would be served than the ordinary *laou tsiew*, made of the *no-me* rice, which has been described above.

THE LANTERN-SELLER.

THE LANTERN-SELLER.

THE chief fault of this drawing is the fewness of the lanterns. The artist has felt obliged to omit more than one-half, in order to bring his picture within reasonable compass. Imagine a thronged thoroughfare, eight feet in its extreme width—much narrowed, however, by the projecting sign-boards of the shops, which are pendent from under the low eaves—and then you will allow that our friend, with his frail cargo, has achieved no small triumph when he has safely piloted his way through the bustling crowds. It has often occurred to me that the lantern-seller, with his light, yet enormously long and cumbrous burden, was a forcible illustration of the mildness and patience of Chinese natural character. Down the street he goes, occupying within a few feet its extreme width, unable to see clearly a-head of him, and yet, beyond an occasional mishap, when at a sudden turn he runs foul of some heedless pedestrian, he

steers clear of all obstacles, and deposits his load
safely at the warehouse. The lanterns here represented are those in ordinary use as hand-lanterns at
night; they are in an unfinished state—in fact,
mere skeletons—made of the finest possible slips of
the Chinese householder's friend, the bamboo, intertwined so as to form a fine network. They are
nearly oval in shape, slightly flattened at the top
and bottom, which are both open. The bottom is
fitted with a spiked socket of wood, on which the
candle is fixed. From four points of this socket
four wires run, which are bent and fastened together through the open top. On the spiked
socket the candle is fixed, and, by means of this
wire, the lantern is carried on a short hooked stick.
The fine network of bamboo is covered with transparent oil-paper, and then painted—sometimes
with grotesque devices, sometimes with objects of
nature, sometimes with a simple motto, but most
frequently with the name of the owner and his
residence, in red letters. In China there is no
gas; and, save the occasional glimmer of a poor
oil lamp, equivalent to a miserable rush-light, at
some gate or bridge, the streets are quite dark;
therefore, no one thinks of steering out at night
without his lantern. Even at the time of full

moon, a prudent man will not venture abroad without it.

A thronged thoroughfare, or a busy wharf, at night presents a curious scene to the stranger's eye, though, like everything else, it ceases to attract notice when once it has become common. There multitudes of gay lanterns are seen dancing along, backwards and forwards; some borne by the chair-bearers, who make their way with marvellous rapidity through opposing obstacles; some dangling easily in the hand of a quiet son of Han, who is on his way to or from a friend's house. In case of a dense crowd, some servant, presuming on his master's authority, will thrust himself forward with the cry, " Make way for the Lo family." Sometimes, by means of the lantern as representative of the house, intimidation is offered, and sums of money are squeezed out of a timid and wealthy citizen. The lanterns of foreigners' houses have not unfrequently been used for this purpose; for great is the fear still of the weight of the arm of the family of the Red-haired.

The lanterns now described are those in ordinary use. Besides these, there is a great variety of all sizes, shapes, and materials. In large houses and mandarin offices an immense round lantern is used;

the framework made of thicker slips of bamboo
than the others, and not, as before, intertwined.
This is usually covered with thin gauze, has inscribed upon it the name of the family or the
office, and hangs in the centre hall of the house.
On occasions of festivity—such as marriage-feasts
—the hall is hung with hexagon or octagon-shaped
lanterns of carved mahogany, ornamented at the
angles with silk tassels, and covered partly with
transparent paper, elegantly painted with scenes of
landscape or historical figures, and the lower part
bound round with crimson crape. There is, besides, a more durable kind made with horn, instead
of paper or gauze. This, however, is clumsy, and
but seldom used. The makers of these lanterns
work up the thin transparent horn in various devices, the most common of which is intended to
represent a carp; the scales of the fish are pieces
of horn dyed red, the head is highly ornamented
with coloured glass or precious stones. These are
seldom found even in the houses of the rich gentry;
for they are expensive, and indeed more ingenious
than elegant.

It is, however, at the " Feast of Lanterns" that
the greatest variety is displayed; and ingenuity is
then taxed to the utmost to devise quaint forms of

animal life. Then you may see children—some
with rabbits on wheels, some with a fish suspended
from a little stick, some with a fair lady in green
appearing from an opening muscle-shell; some,
again, with the gay-winged butterfly, or the green
locust; some with a nondescript and very formid-
able-looking animal, something like a tiger. For a
week previous and subsequent to the day of the
feast, these appear in front of their houses playing
with their pretty illuminated toys. It is on this
occasion that a peculiar kind of lantern is seen,
which does not make its appearance at other times.
It is called the *tsow-ma-tung*, and deserves a notice
for the ingenuity of its construction. The draught
of air caused by the heat of the lighted candles
within causes the rapid revolution of an horizontal
wheel fixed on a pivot. This wheel has light and
almost invisible threads of silk attached to different
parts of its circumference, and these are fastened
again to the loose heads, arms, legs, wings, &c., of
figures of men, women, horses, insects, &c., which
are portrayed on the outside. As the wheel
revolves, the threads will of course raise their legs,
arms, wings, &c., which fall again as it slackens;
so that we have ladies and gentlemen bowing to
each other, horses prancing, birds flapping their

wings, and various similar ingenious movements. The dexterity of the contrivance is shown in the regularity with which the threads work; they never become entangled, but will move night after night, for a month together, without getting out of order. The best of these are rather expensive; but as they are only intended for occasional use on this feast, they are seldom made with that profuse carving and ornament which causes the larger lanterns of the Chinese to reach some tens, or even hundreds, of dollars in value. As this is a great time of festivity, the exterior of the house, as well as the interior, is illuminated. This is often done by means of the "centipede." It consists, like its fellow, the "dragon," of a number of large lanterns strung together. It is then hung on a tall pole, and as the long body sways to and fro in the wind, the peculiar wriggling movement of the scolopendron is accurately represented.

When the animal of good omen, the mild and majestic "dragon," is carried in procession, each joint of his huge frame is formed by a lighted lantern set on a pole, and carried by a man. As the long many-jointed beast winds about in the villages, and rears his head, terrible with open jaws, amid the clang of gongs, and the fizzing and cracking of squibs, and the shouts of an excited populace, one can but feel that he is sojourning in a strange country, and is brought into contact with strange scenes.

CHINESE LANTERNS.

CHINESE BOOKSELLER.

祝念先生

—

THE TAOUIST PRIEST EXORCISING.

—◆—

TAOUISM, like some other religions of the world, has degenerated into a vile superstition. We recognize in its present form none of those great ideas which stamped its first appearance. It seems to be literally rotting away from within—tumbling to pieces by its own decay.

Originally Taouism was contemplative; it studied retirement rather than action, and, like its rival Buddhism, taught that the most perfect man was he who retired most within himself, and kept furthest aloof from all the interests of social life.

In its first great utterances, made by its founder, Laou-tsze, the immediate forerunner of Confucius, we hear tell, in simple yet grand language, of some invisible principle (called Taou) which, while itself existing alone, pervades in its secret influence all things, absolute and undivided, without motion, will, or form.

This same ancient classic has startled Europeans

by the use of language similar to that of the
apostle John, the more so as the term Taou is
equivalent to his *Logos*, or Word : "All things (it
says) were made by Taou, and nothing made that
was not made by it." It has also amazed some
Christian divines by speaking of "the three pure,"
by which some have been led, with greater haste
than judgment, to assert that the doctrine of the
Trinity was known and taught in China for at
least five centuries before the Christian era.

Few, however, even of the Taouist priesthood,
now understand or enunciate its principles. What
Chinese Buddhism is to the original teachings of
Gautama, such Taouism is to the original utterances of its founder. Its priests pore in secret
over the works of a mystical and unreal alchemy;
they worship, with solemn services, certain stars
which control the destinies of life and death;
they hold converse with the dead; they deal in
potent spells and incantations—and so pander to
the vulgar taste in its cravings for the marvellous.

Taouism, as at present in action, is best described
by an individual example. When any member of
a family is dangerously ill, and other remedies have
failed, a bevy of the priests of Taou is called in,
that they may exercise their art in expelling the

evil spirit, which is supposed to have taken possession, and to be feeding upon the body of the
sufferer. Nothing is more common than, on passing a house at night, to hear the drums and flutes
and loudly-chanted prayers proceeding from the
centre hall of the dwelling. On entering, you
would see loose-robed priests, wearing high black
caps, with solemn mien, performing unintelligible
acts of mystic ritual. The noise of these worshippers is to us most distressing; and it is a wonder
how the sick person can endure, for several hours
in the night, such a continual succession of most
discordant sounds, finished up soon after midnight
by the firing of hundreds of small crackers, the
report of large popguns, the clanging of gongs,
and the bellowing of huge conchs. He is probably
reconciled to it by the belief that he is receiving
benefit, and that the evil spirit will by these means
be expelled from his body.

The whole service is a curious mixture of bribery
and intimidation. Food of various kinds is plenti-
fully provided, and spread in the house; and certainly, if the spirit were in any way allied to flesh
and blood, the rich pork, and sappy eel, and well-
cooked poultry, might be supposed to have more
charms than the lungs, or heart, or intestines of a

diseased human being. The old proverb, however, " de gustibus," &c., still holds good; the laws of taste are not amenable to logic; and lest the spirit's morbid appetite should still induce him, raven-like, to prefer as food the human subject, the noisy squibs, and clanging gongs, and potent spells of prayer are employed to intimidate and drive him away from his usurped tenement.

Our engraving represents one of these Taouist priests in the act of thus exorcising a spirit. The young man kneeling by his side has come to consult him on behalf of a sick parent or relative; a charm, consisting of some scroll of mysterious writing, signed, it may be, by the prince of demons, is lying on the stool in front of the table. The *muh-yu*, found in all Buddhist temples, which is struck rapidly when prayer is recited, is ready to his right hand. He is dipping his finger into a cup of tea, and is about to sprinkle it in a circle before him. His manual of prayer is open by his side; two red candles are burning on the table, which is furnished with a hanging of yellow silk or satin. Both the worshippers wear their hats; for in China, as generally throughout Asia, the head covered with the hat or turban of ceremony is a sign of respect.

Were we to judge from their outward demeanor, we should say that these persons were, many of them, much in earnest; and like Dr. Livingstone's rain-makers in South Africa, that they were not wilful impostors, but rather have first so thoroughly deceived themselves as to believe that they are not deceiving others. This is the only way in which we can satisfactorily explain many of the phenomena in the religion of heathen nations.

The ramifications of Taouist superstition are very intricate, and only one thoroughly initiated in the mysteries of this faith could adequately describe them. To us they appear a mere tissue of absurdities; and if we ever have patience to pursue our inquiry on any particular point to the end, we find that, phantom-like, it eludes us just when we seem to be grasping it. The firm strong hand of science clutches at it, and it proves a shadow.

How far there is any reality about these various superstitions in heathen lands, and how far the personal agency of evil is employed in them, will probably continue for a long time open to discussion. In my opinion, wilful fraud or irrational credulity will account for at least nine-tenths of all supernatural marvels.

When I see pamphlets by educated men, clergy-
men of our own Church, written to prove that table-
turning is a reality, and hear them profess to have
held actual communication, by means of a manipu-
lated table, with the spirits of departed men, I am
not surprised to find that the power of holding
conference with the unseen world is claimed as a
real power by Taouist exorcists. Necromancy is a
subject which, in every country and in every age,
has had its advocates—it is still practised in America, in England, in France, in Germany, and probably many other countries even of the Christian-
ized world; and the Taouist priests naturally take
advantage of the belief of the Chinese people, that
communication with the dead is practicable, and
willingly help them to extract secrets from the
region beyond the grave.

I must not conclude this paper without mention-
ing a most remarkable fact about modern Taouism.
In the province of Keangsoo, the head of this
religion holds his court, and exercises a wide-spread,
and most extraordinary influence, almost rivalling
that of the Pope with his college of cardinals. Before any deity in the Palladian temple of any *Heen*
city throughout China can exercise his functions,
he must receive his appointment under the seal of

this spiritual ruler. When we remember that these cities, more than 1200 in number, occupy different centres throughout the eighteen provinces of China, or in other words that 360 millions of people come more or less under their influence, and that these Palladian temples more than any others, on every new and full moon, attract the worship of the people, and that the mandarins go chiefly here to worship, we may gather an idea of the significance of the fact we have in one brief line above stated.

The person who holds this office and disposes thus of his spiritual patronage is called *Tseang Teen sze;* that is, his family name is *Tseang,* his name, which descends to that one of his children who is to succeed him in office, is *Teen sze,* or "the messenger of heaven." For more than a thousand years has this family been exercising their ecclesiastical functions. One of the commonest stories about him is, that he has control over certain malignant spirits which enter the bodies of women and cause grievous diseases; these, on accusation made against them and on payment of a sum of money, he is bound to exorcise.

Many other marvellous tales are related of this man and of his doings—tales which provoke a smile, and would seem fit matter for ridicule and a butt for the shafts of satire, were they not so implicitly believed.

I have often longed to wander off in the direction of this arch-priest's sanctuary, and try whether the huge jars in his court, which are said to contain these spirits, would bear heretical sight and touch. I have also often longed to know whether the mark on the body, which distinguishes that one of the family who is to succeed his father in his office, is visible to mortal eye; to test, in short, any one of the thousand miraculous powers assigned to him. Such a journey would, however, be profitless. I should, after all, see or learn but little more than I have seen or learnt. The chanting of prayers, the offering of cups of tea or wine, tables covered with food, scrolls of mysterious writing, genuflexions and manual signs, would meet the eye and ear; and when told that some spirit of evil had been exorcised by these charms—that some idol had received his spiritual promotion—I should still be obliged to draw upon my faith for assent. It is the Master's hand alone that can put together the disjointed puzzle of the human mind. Taouist and Buddhist fables will be alike believed till the pure faith of the Gospel exercises its rightful dominion.

THE BLIND SEER.

THE BLIND SEER.

THIS is a touching picture. It is the type of a
large class of persons in China. Blindness, a
malady from which no country is wholly exempt,
is peculiarly common in the land of Han. The
frequency, however, of this affliction, is not to be
attributed to any special climatical influences, nor
to anything in the habits of the people; but rather
to neglect, or to ignorance of sound curative methods when the eye has been attacked by disease.
Her people neither gaze upon eternal snows, nor
have they to traverse boundless plains of scorching
sand. If China be far behind the medical science
of Europe in the skill of her oculists, she has,
however, long anticipated Christendom in finding
scope for the exercise of the mental energies of the
blind. Systematic efforts to impart education to
this class are but of late date in Europe. With
the glorious exception of the hospital for the blind,
founded in Paris about the year 1260, by St.

Louis, for the relief of his soldiers who lost their
sight during his Egyptian expedition, little had
been done for the blind. The general inefficiency
and moral corruption prevailing in this hospital led
the philanthropic Haüy to attempt to do for the
blind what the Abbé de l'Epée had done for the deaf
and dumb. By his efforts a noble institution was
founded, in which those who were thus afflicted
were taught the most useful arts and sciences of
civilized life. Within the last fifty years various
institutions have been opened, with more or less
success, in the different countries of Europe; and
now France, England, Russia, Holland, Denmark,
Germany, and Switzerland can all boast similar
hospitals or schools for the blind. Before that
period their condition was lamentable indeed.
Being taught no trade, they were compelled, if
poor, to become common beggars in the streets;
and if removed above such a misfortune, they were
yet completely dependent upon others for the
cultivation of their mental faculties. Consequently,
those vivid perceptions, which the very loss of sight
stimulated into action, remained, save in a very
few cases of rare talent and energy, altogether un-
improved. In China, however, as we have said,
this class of persons had, from a very early period,

found scope for the exercise of their mental powers. Whether from that extraordinary clearness of intellectual perception which usually distinguishes the blind, or from their attention being no longer distracted by outward and visible objects, they have been supposed to possess the power of looking into the unseen world. Hence, as our title suggests, the corporeally blind has become, in the Chinese estimation, mentally a seer. This is, indeed, their recognized and legitimate calling; and, without any of those refined appliances which have been devised by us and other nations, for the teaching of the blind, they have managed, from dictation or mutual instruction, to commit to memory several volumes which have reference to their secret art. The memory of the blind is proverbially strong; a remarkable instance of which is given by one of the Jesuit missionaries, who relates, that in Japan the records of the country are committed to their care—in which case a digest, at least, of the whole history of the country must be stored in their mind.

Our picture accurately represents one of these blind seers, led by a little boy, going his rounds in the pursuit of his profession. Those few Chinese words, written on a board and suspended from his viol, state that he will "truly prognosticate, and use no satanic deception." He would be regarded by a stranger as a mere beggar; for beggar-like he thrums his guitar, and makes melancholy music to attract the notice of the bystanders. Blind beggars there are among the Chinese; but they do not employ the viol or guitar, they only sit or kneel on the hard pavement, striking their forehead on the ground, and uttering doleful cries of distress to excite pity and obtain relief. The fortune-teller having thus elicited attention, is frequently invited to a house, and there, after hearing from the family the matter upon which information is desired, and submitting a few needful questions, he will take up his guitar, and gradually becoming inspired with his theme, will pour forth, in disconnected passages from his books, or in wild rhapsodies of his own composing, those thoughts which are to guide the family to a solution of their perplexity. The matter of consultation is of course as varied as are the phases of human sorrow and anxiety. Very frequently a relation, it may be a father or a husband, has been a long while absent, and no tidings of him have been heard. Domestic anxiety is therefore relieved, and bright hopes are suggested by the outpourings of prophetic song. Occasionally, however, there seems to be a foreboding of calamity, and then dark **and** dismal are the strains by which **the** coming misfortune of the house is foreshadowed. When children are born blind, **or have** become blind **in** their early infancy, they **are most** frequently apprenticed to their seniors in the profession, and commit to memory those stores of recondite learning which the master imparts out of his own mental treasury. **First a** line, then a page, then a chapter, and then **a** volume, is laid by in that capacious repository; and **by** the age of thirty, or even before, they are prepared to go forth and **earn** their own livelihood. A blind seer who stands **high in** his profession is in **easy** comfortable circumstances; he usually **occupies a** room fronting the street, **and** makes his calling **known by means** of a sign-board, trusting to the passers-by **for employ**ment. **I have frequently** conversed with **such** blind seers, and **found them** very intelligent, and **fully** answering to their proverbial **character of** mental activity. They listened with marked interest to **the story of the Redeemer; and I could but feel that had their eyes been opened by His** gracious **hand, they would, as in** the days of His human **ministry, have followed Him** gladly **in the** way and sung His praise. **A few blind persons** who have come under the influence of foreigners are being taught to read their own mother tongue. By private liberality a manual is now in course of preparation for teaching the dialect of Ningpo by the embossed books; while at the same time that great public benefactor, the British and Foreign Bible Society, is preparing the Gospel of St. Luke for their instruction in the elements of Divine truth. We can only say of all such efforts for the alleviation of the poor and afflicted, whether at home or abroad, may God speed them, and direct them to a favourable issue; and even if those efforts result not in the success anticipated, may they at least return with a blessing into the bosom of their advocates.

THE BLIND DIVINER.

DR. MORRISON says, "the Chinese have two methods of divination: one by means of sixty-four slips of wood, the other by casting three coins from a tortoise-shell box."

The former of these is very common in all Buddhist temples, and is resorted to daily by thousands of people; the latter is seldom seen in the north, it may be more frequently employed in the south of China. The number of these "sticks of fate" (as they are sometimes called) is determined by the eight times eight, or sixty-four enigmatical diagrams, which form the basis of that most ancient and perplexing of all the Chinese classics, called the *Yih-king*. Consultation by means of these is one of the commonest incidents of the Chinaman's life, when he feels perplexed about the unknown future, and is anxious to dive into its dark secrets. The box in which they are contained is formed of a section of bamboo about eight inches high; the knot in the stem forms a natural bottom to the box, the top is left open. The "sticks" are thin smooth slips of bamboo, about ten inches long; on each of them a short sentence of doubtful import is written, in which the answer to the inquiry is supposed to be contained. The person consulting takes the box in both hands, stands in the presence of the idol whom he has invoked, and by whose kindly influence he looks to obtain a right answer of guidance in his perplexity; he then shakes the box rapidly, turning its mouth gradually downwards, till one or more of the slips shows a tendency to separate from the rest, and to leap out. After a minute or so, the shaking being more and more carefully performed, one of them works its way beyond the others, and falls out; the rest are immediately tossed back, the slip which has fallen to the ground is picked up, and by the sentence inscribed upon it the desired answer is obtained. The method of divining by arrows, alluded to in Ezekiel's prophecy (Ezek. xxi. 21), has by some been considered a similar mode of divination to this. They imagine that the polished shafts of the arrow had each a significant sentence inscribed, and by *drawing* one of these from the quiver, instead of shaking them out in the manner described above, the needed direction was obtained.*

Our picture represents the second method, performed by means of three copper coins cast upon the table from a shell box. This coin called *Tung-tseen*, or copper money, is the only issue from the Chinese mint. These coins vary much in size and appearance, some being about as large as a farthing and well-executed, others again not bigger or thicker than a sixpence, the edges rough, and the inscription almost illegible. They are all pierced with a square hole, by means of which

---

* There is an interesting note on this subject in the "Illustrated Commentary on the Old and New Testament." (Charles Knight & Co., Ludgate Street.) On the sentence "He made his arrows bright," in the 21st verse of the 21st chapter of Ezekiel, the writer remarks : Here is a clear reference to the very widely diffused ancient superstition of Belomancy, or divination by arrows. The most common process was to mark a number of arrows with the names of the nations or places, which were the subject of consideration. The arrows were then shaken together in a quiver, and the marks on the one first drawn forth decided the preference. Not unlike it was a method in use among the Arabs. The arrows were three in number : upon one of them was written, "Command me, Lord ;" upon the second, "Forbid, or prevent, Lord ;" and the third was blank. These were put into a bag, which was held by the diviner, by whom also the lot was drawn. If the first was drawn, it conveyed an affirmative response ; the second intimated a negative ; and when the blank arrow appeared, a second drawing was made.

they are carried, a thousand on a double string, divided off with a simple knot into hundreds for the convenience of counting. Each coin has on one face the name in Chinese of the reigning sovereign, together with the date of its coinage, and on the obverse a sentence in *Manchow*, to show under whose yoke of authority the nation at present subsists. The accompanying sketch gives both these faces.

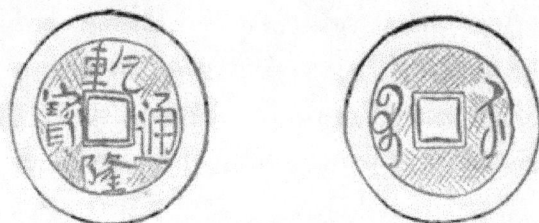

By means of these "*cash*" (for such is their foreign name), the blind man of our picture is prophesying of things to come to the meek and rather stupid-looking youth, who has come to consult him; and not a little influence will the few words, uttered by the blind seer, have upon his fears or hopes of the unknown future.

In the former sketch I have more fully described the occupation of the blind, and the means by which they usually obtain their living. I will only say here, that the divining-room of these seers, or

diviners, is seldom empty. The mind, unguided by
the pole-star of Revelation, and ever tossed upon
the sea of doubt, gladly makes for any haven that
promises rest, and deludes itself into the belief
that it finds it in these prophesyings of ignorant
soothsayers. The anxieties of life afford occasions
enough for the employment of the soothsayer and
his arts; and if history and experience tell us that
Revelation itself has hardly sufficed to eradicate from
men's minds the irrational and unholy cravings of
superstitious curiosity, should we be surprised to
find them rampant among the votaries of Buddha,
and the worshippers of dumb idols? The small
bronze censer, containing fragrant sticks of incense,
is always placed (as in our sketch) on the table,
between the two candlesticks. This incense is the
invariable accompaniment of every religious ceremony, and is found constantly burning before every
idol shrine.

At the back of the table, which stands against
the wall, are the usual hanging scrolls, containing
some sentences bearing upon the diviner's art. In
this case the words run thus: "Before you consult
the diviner, you are already three-parts master of
your position. In determining and arranging, first
reckon the means you have in hand," or, in other

words, " count the cost." Such sentences are certainly eminently safe, well leavened with not a little worldly wisdom, reminding us of those oracular responses from ancient shrines, where either some general principles of action were laid down, or some answer of ambiguous import was framed. Alas! how hard does it seem to induce man to fight his way to the noble responsibility of thought! How easily and naturally does he betake himself instead to omens for good and evil, obtained, as in the case of our sketch, by the configuration of the three copper coins cast by the diviner on the table!

A ROADSIDE ALTAR.

針匠

THE NEEDLE-MAKER.

POPULAR tradition in England has informed us that the Chinese make their needles by filing down iron crowbars; and the fact is referred to as an illustration of their patience and perseverance. The Chinaman who heard this would doubtless feel that we were complimenting him upon the possession of some good qualities at the expense of others; for in commending his patience and perseverance, we should not say much for his ingenuity and contrivance.

Probably a hoax was played upon some simple-minded foreigner, who, as he passed down the street, took notice of that common sight, a man engaged in filing an iron rod, and gathered from him the interesting information that a needle would be the eventual result of his toil. Worse mistakes than this have been made; for instance, Monsieur Huc tells us, with great gravity, that the people in the north of China *gamble for their fingers* when all their money is gone, and that the losing party deliberately chops off one of his digits with a small sharp hatchet, cauterizes the stump, and proceeds with his game. This ridiculous account is evidently founded upon the near resemblance in sound of two Chinese phrases, " to chop off a finger," and " to draw a lot," which is a common mode of gambling.

As I am about to give the reader a little interesting information (*i.e.* as interesting as the subject in hand will allow) about Chinese needle-making, I must beg his attention first to the kindred subject of pins. The Chinese are as much at fault about our pins as we are about their chopsticks, or any other article the exact use of which we have misapprehended. They invariably mistake the pin for its first cousin the needle, the chief difference being (as they say) that one has a head without an eye, and the other an eye without a head; they express their surprise how the thread is fastened, how the little knob at the top can be brought through the stitch hole. They never saw a pin until introduced by foreigners : hence their ignorant mistake. It is not a little singular, and suggests at once the remarkable difference which must exist between their and our tailors' work, and Chinese and European ladies' and children's dresses, that while about *twenty millions* of pins daily issue from our manufactories, for home and foreign consumption, not a single pin finds any employment among the Chinese. It will be an auspicious day for the pin-trade when China's millions shall use pins instead of tapes to fasten ladies' dresses; for if twenty millions of these little articles are required for the use of only a part of Europe, a very simple rule-of-three sum would give the required amount for the 360 millions of China proper.

By the way, before I quite throw the subject of pins aside, let me just ask, did it ever occur to any of our gentle sisters in Europe that they are responsible for the daily consumption of these twenty millions of pins? A pin seems as though it might last for ever. Unless violently beheaded, or bent, blunted, or lost, it continues still the same neat, straight piece of sharpened wire which it was when it left the hands of the manufacturer. There is something startling in the thought that, day by day throughout the year, the existing number of pins should have been increasing at this enormous ratio, and yet that it never appears that we have one too many. At a critical moment, when a pin is most of all needed, it is frequently the most difficult thing to find.

It is believed that the needles about equal the pins in number. By the aid of a machine of six-horse power, the immense number of fourteen millions may be made in one week; and though there are hundreds of such machines at work, the supply only keeps pace with the demand.

In China, where the use of the needle is as common as it is with ourselves, and where no machinery exists to assist in the manufacture, how vast must be the number of hands employed in this one branch of trade! Many, doubtless, would deprecate the introduction of intricate machinery, or consider it a questionable benefit; for though it might be maintained that the increase of mechanical power would but call into operation latent energies, and increase the material prosperity of the working classes, still it is a fact that at present a large proportion of the teeming population of the land find employment, and earn sufficient wages for subsistence, by needle-making. That part of the process which consists in boring the eye is one of the commonest sights which strikes the foreigner's attention as he passes down the street where these artizans are plying their trade. It is well represented in our picture. The instrument by which it is effected is simple and ingenious. It consists of a slender polished upright shaft, about the thickness of an arrow, pointed with a very small speck of diamond; this passes through a circular hole in a flat horizontal piece of wood, from the two extremities of which a cord is attached, which is fastened to a knob at the top of the shaft. Then, by the simple movement of the hand up and down, a regular spinning movement is communicated to the diamond-pointed borer, the cord winds round the shaft backwards and forwards, as in the spinning-mills of our nurseries, and the needle being laid in a groove a few seconds suffices to make the eyelet hole. Though this instrument is represented, in our picture, in the needle-maker's hand, yet a separate drawing may convey a clearer idea of it to the reader.

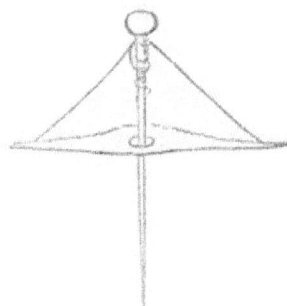

A Chinese needle bears, as might be expected, a great resemblance to its foreign sister. One of

Pestalozzi's teachers might hold one up to her class of juveniles, and make the same object-lesson from it, as from one taken out of her own needle-book; still, it has its peculiar characteristics, and minute examination will discover many differences. First (like the people), it is short: the Chinese tailor and sempstress prefer a stumpy needle; they say they can work more quickly with it. Again: it is plainer than ours; it has not had the same care expended upon it; the head is not flattened, but the eye is bored in the round wire, no neat groove is cut to make room for the thread. Our needle, in fact, like almost all our articles of manufacture, bears the impress of the progress of the last fifty years; the Chinese needle, on the contrary, has known no change for the last twenty centuries.

The needle-maker is a member of a very poor and hard-working class. No parent, save from sheer necessity, would bring up a child to this trade. Still, it has produced its great men; many a little boy who would have ground needle points, and bored needle-eyes for his working life in his father's shop, has risen by genius and application to eminence among his countrymen. It has not fallen to my lot personally to meet with such an one. But I do know one, who, under the influence of the same mysterious power which wrought upon the simple fishermen of Galilee, manfully girt up his loins to follow the Divine Saviour. The poor needle-maker entwined himself round my heart with the affection of a brother; he has been called from his shop and from his toil. I saw him last in the cold grasp of death, yet with his mind awake to his Saviour's presence; and I afterwards committed his body to the ground in the full assurance of life and immortality. His mud-floor cottage is now lit up by the faith of the Gospel. His widow and child, who survive him, are walking in his footsteps.

HUSBANDMAN.

A TEA-PICKER.

賣

花

THE FLORIST.

THE Chinese must be a strange people, from the very varying accounts which are given of them by different observers. They are over-estimated in some things, and undervalued in others, misunderstood in most. Take the matter of flowers. We are accustomed to consider them a nation of horticulturists on a small scale. Is it not the prevalent idea in England, that the houses are surrounded with a neat piece of garden-ground, which is cultivated with great care, and shows some rare flowers as the fruit of patient, kindly toil? Let the reader honestly say whether such has not hitherto been his notion of this canny, thrifty people of the Eastern continent. Now, what are the facts? If any one were to go to China, he might search a whole province through, and not find anything round the dwelling-houses which answered even to a decent European garden. In a garden, we picture to ourselves nicely-cut and elegantly-shaped beds,

filled with bright-hued flowers; raised terraces, or
gravel-walks, where visitors may go and admire
the productions of the season; perhaps a spreading
tree, or shady arbour, offering a welcome and cool
retreat during the hot days of summer. Anything
like this he will seek for in vain in China; but
in its place, among the poorer classes, a few pots
of flowers in the open court; and amongst the
gentry, a small yard at the side or back of the
building, where is displayed some dwarfed fir, no
bigger than a doll's Christmas-tree; some gnarled
camphor, rising no higher than a good-sized cauli-
flower; and a few carefully-cultivated plants, whose
flowers are forced into gigantic size by a peculiar
method of cultivation and the copious application
of manure. The nursery-gardens, often visited
and described by foreigners, contain many such
specimens; they have no more beauty than the
covered stalls of Covent Garden Market, but
merely contain rows of pots, filled with the plants
just coming into flower, ranged for the convenience
of sale. The plants which are in the ground are
merely seedlings, which will be transplanted, not
into the parterres of country gardens, but into
small pots to occupy their place on a stand in the
court-yards or rooms of houses.

My assertion of the absence of what we call gardens will be borne out by all those who know the country. One fact may serve to convince the general reader that I have not exaggerated.

In the large city of Ningpo, whose walls are five miles in circumference, and whose population numbers nearly half a million of inhabitants, there are only two gardens which are ever thought worthy of a visit from foreigners. They belong to the Kang and the Le families respectively. The larger and better of these consists of a piece of ground about 90 feet long by 30 wide, most ingeniously "fitted up" with rock-work, and a tiny pool of water, to resemble mountain scenery in miniature. From between the fissures of the rock, costly plants have been made to grow; others appear (in the usual way) in pots, set upon a flower-stand. This is all one of the finest second-class cities in the empire has to show of pleasure-grounds. In the island of Chusan there is a garden about twice the size of this, even more ingeniously arranged: arches are formed by the rock-work, intricate passages wind round behind it, you ascend and descend by small staircases of stone steps, openings are made here and there to afford a view of the pretty court and the quaintly-curved and

H

ornamented roofs which adjoin; a kind of summer-house, with elegant lattice-work, invites you to a shady seat. When our troops were occupying the island of Chusan, this spot, situated within a convenient walk from the barracks, became so great an object of attraction to the officers and others, that the proprietor (a wealthy Chinaman), pestered with the daily calls of visitors, fled the place, and ever after kept an old and trusty steward to do the honours of the house in his absence. Tea is liberally supplied to all visitors, and, as in the case of show-houses at home, a gratuity is left with the servants for their trouble.

From what has thus been said, it will be readily understood that the Chinese do not value those flowers which group well, forming massy patches, but only those which show well in a pot. They have found fault with several of our European introductions, such as the coreopsis and zinnia, because of their tendency to form large and unwieldy plants. They admired the separate flowers much, but could turn them to little account. Even the dahlia they would find difficult to reduce to the proper dimensions. The ranunculus, the pansy, the geranium, the cactus, or the hyacinth, they exceedingly esteem and admire.

The figure in our engraving needs but little description. It is simply that of a small market-gar-
dener, carrying about for sale those plants which
he has reared in his little bit of nursery ground.
He seems very familiar to my eyes, from having
seen such a one continually passing my door.
As we became acquainted, he would leave with me
some plant of native growth, while I gave him in
exchange any exotic which had secured for itself a
footing in its new home.

I dare not write much about flowers, when so
full an account has already been given in the
pages of Fortune, who for many years toiled hard
in collecting his specimens from every part of the
country. Any one who desires to know what
the country has or has not in the way of plants,
both wild and cultivated, had better consult his
pages.

Many an estate, a hundred years hence, will
have to acknowledge a debt of gratitude to his
exertions, when the lovely cypresses and firs,
brought by him into this country, have reared
on high their luxuriant heads, and displayed their
golden cones to the admiring gaze of our children's
children.

HEMP PALM.

No. 16.

賣鴉片

THE OPIUM-SMOKER.

THE OPIUM-SMOKER.

——◆——

THE English wife and mother vents many a deep curse upon alcohol; some of our philanthropists would fain see it confined, like other green, red, and blue liquids, in the bulky bottles of the druggists' shops. The Chinese wife and mother utters an equally hearty imprecation upon opium, and the efforts of their philanthropists are directed to its exclusion from the marts of ordinary commerce, to take its place among other rare and potent poisons which the skill of man has made serviceable to the alleviation or the cure of disease.

Tobacco and opium are two products which have spread in China with marvellous rapidity. Not many centuries since the former was unknown; smoking was a crime punishable with death. The Chinese Emperors joined with sovereigns of Europe and popes of Rome in execrating this narcotic, and punishing the growers of the weed, or the vendors of the leaf, with excommunication or death. The same quaint reason for the prohibition has been everywhere alleged—namely, that " men appeared like devils emitting smoke from their mouth and nostrils." Now, a crowd of Chinamen shows a forest of tobacco-pipes, and the perfumed smoke curls in graceful wreaths even from the women's lips.

The history of the opium trade is too well known to need repetition. Commencing about the year 1770 with 200 chests, which were admitted as a medicinal drug on payment of a certain im- post, in less than a hundred years it has increased *seven or eight hundred* fold, for at present 80,000 chests are the annual importation from British India alone ; while the cultivation of the poppy and the manufacture of opium is carried on to an unknown extent on Chinese soil. Those who have attempted, from imperfect data, to make a calcu- lation have judged that at least an equal amount is raised from the native provinces. Nor is the limit yet reached ; when 160,000 chests are divided among 360,000,000 of people, it will be found that, according to the average quantity which every smoker consumes, not more than a very small per- centage of the whole population have as yet availed themselves of this luxury. There must be something in the constitution of the Chinaman, or in his climate, which predisposes him to this evil habit. It would never fasten itself upon an active, energetic, enterprising people, unless some such predisposing cause assisted. Our national sin is that of drunkenness. We have always been a hard-drinking people; our northern ancestors found their delight in deep potations. Even less than half a century ago, an ordinary dinner-party would not unfrequently be crowned by such orgies as never now disfigure polite society. The Chinaman does not refuse wine, but he does not make it his bane; he has generally sense enough to know when he has had enough. The streets occasionally present the spectacle of a "red-eyed" man, the sure sign of partial inebriation; but they do not afford those disgraceful exhibitions of reeling men, either made senseless or infuriated with drink. The quiet soothing opium has a greater charm; under its fatal spell the mild son of Han more readily succumbs—its effect accords with his own natural temperament, which rather leads to patience and love of peace than to rude blows and fighting.

As there is still much ignorance among foreigners as to the nature of opium-smoking, it may be worth while to describe both how it originates, and what are its effects. The common idea seems to be, that men take a pipe of opium much as a person indulges in excess of wine, merely for the pleasure which the intoxicating fumes give. But this is no just comparison. We may rather liken the opium-smoker to the habitual dram-drinker, whose depraved and vitiated appetite now craves of him the powerful stimulant. Indeed, dram-drinking and opium-smoking are very much on a par, though the latter is on many accounts preferable, chiefly as being less brutalizing. Opium does not excite, as do gin and brandy, the ferocious passions of men, but rather, by enervating, soothes its victim. The habit is easily acquired. It commences mostly in one of two ways: either it is resorted to as a remedy for some disease (heartburn, for instance, which it immediately relieves), or it is first taken at late hours in dissolute company for the sake of producing wakefulness and forced energy. In both cases a fortnight's use of the drug is sufficient to tie the habit, like a millstone, round the neck, when nothing but almost superhuman effort will avail to cast it off. The gnawing agony of the unsatisfied craving is maddening; besides which there is a prostration of all physical strength, the eyes are weak and watery, the mouth runs with saliva, the mind itself has become weakened; and, in the presence of all this suffering, there is the certainty of relief a few seconds after the opium-pipe has touched the lips —a relief which lasts perhaps half, perhaps only the third or fourth part of the day, when the same craving again comes round. The opium-smoker, when confirmed in his habit, just anticipates this craving; and, if he be a man of infirm purpose, who has but little moral strength, he will fly to his pipe on the first symptoms of faintness or nausea, and so make a more frequent recurrence to the stimulant necessary. Cases have been known where men of strong determination have with one mighty effort thrown off the habit, which was threatening them with ruin; such, however, are very rare. Both body and mind are usually too weak for the execution of the purpose. Dysentery and other diseases at once threaten the life of the confirmed opium-smoker who would renounce his vice; and, as we have shown, the mind is unable to endure the fearful struggle which the renunciation of the habit entails. Widely-differing estimates have been formed of the proportion of opium-smokers in China; by some they are set

as low as only one or two per cent., by others as
high as eight or ten per cent. of the population.
The deaths also which this poison causes are
variously estimated. Some have made the extreme
assertion that every opium-smoker is sent to his
grave in an average of ten years. We must not,
however, suppose that every smoker who dies has
been killed by opium; for it will be found that
some, had it not been for opium, would have died
much sooner. I do not assert that some better
remedy could not have been found, but only that
the drug has been used as a medicine, and has
stayed the progress of disease. Opium, in the
form of laudanum, is still resorted to by Europeans
for many cases of severe illness; and it would not
be considered fair to say, in case of death, that
opium had killed the patient, though very likely
there is, did we but know it, some safer and better
mode of treatment. The curse of the habit, like
that of drunkenness, falls with especial weight on
the poor. A labouring man is obliged to expend
about one-half of his wages in this single article.
We can at once imagine (though, alas! experience,
rather than imagination, is here our teacher) the
misery which this must cause. If a man earns his
ten shillings a week, and brings home but five, and

has besides ruined his constitution, and incapaci-
tated himself for continuous work, it requires no
spirit of prophecy to tell to what state his family
will soon be reduced. And if once a person who
has enslaved himself to opium loses a situation, he
will find it no easy matter to obtain another; and
then no alternative but the lowest toadyism, theft,
or beggary will be left to him. I have heard a
foreign merchant, himself largely engaged in the
trade, express his firm resolve that no opium-
smoker should remain a servant in his "hong."
The reason is manifest: the moral perception is
blunted by the indulgence, and, what is still more
to the purpose, three times on an average every
day the servant, or *shroff*, or book-keeper, is for a
time unfitted for his work.

The impossibility of casting off the habit when
once it has obtained a firm hold has been before
mentioned, and it may be further illustrated by
the following fact, which was related to me. A
small salesman, or pedlar, was seen toiling along
with great difficulty through the gates of Ningpo,
as if straining every nerve to reach some desired
point; he was seen to stagger and to fall, and his
bundle flew before him out of his reach. While

many passed by, some good Samaritan comes to
him, lifts up his head, and asks what is the matter,
and what he can do for him? He has just strength
to whisper out, "My good friend, please to untie
that bundle; you will find a small box in the
centre; give me two or three of the pills which are
in it, and I shall be all right." It was soon done;
the opium pills had their desired effect, and he
was soon able to rise and pursue his journey to
his inn. This most graphically describes the extreme state of exhaustion which comes on if the
usual period of taking the pipe has passed by.
The pedlar thought, no doubt, he had strength
just to reach his inn, when he would have thrown
himself upon a bed, and called for the opium
pipe; but he miscalculated, by a few minutes, his
powers of endurance, and the pills, (often resorted
to in like cases of extremity), when supplied him
by his friend, perhaps saved him from an untimely
end. Very similar scenes have happened to foreigners travelling in sedan chairs through the
country; the bearers have been obliged to stop
and take a little of the opium, prepared in this form,
in order to prevent complete exhaustion. A long
hour or more, in the middle of the day, has fre-

quently to be allowed, nominally for the sake of dinner and rest, but really, in some instances, for the sake of the opium pipe.

Eloquent tongues and pens have argued the question of the opium traffic. Most opposite have been the conclusions to which they have come. "Opium," says Mr. Crawford, "does not do men much harm; opium-smokers live, many of them, to a great age." "Opium," says Mr. Tait, "as taken by the Chinese, has lost all its medicinal qualities, and leaves only those which are destructive of life; the poison, taken into the lungs, utterly destroys the human system, and sends a man to his grave in an average of ten years." "Opium," Mr. Crawford very positively states, "is no hindrance to legitimate trade with China." "The Chinese," says Mr. Tait, "are losing their health and habits of industry; they are also being drained of their wealth. There are few left to buy your exports, there will be fewer still; the rich produce that should pay for them goes to purchase opium. The trade utterly paralyses legitimate commerce."* Though these latter statements are very strong, they are certainly, by

---

* See "China and its Trade," a pamphlet. Crossley and Billington, Rugby.

the testimony of all, except, perhaps, the opium-merchants themselves, nearer to the truth than the former. A merchant has a very arduous and up-hill struggle whose house refuses to deal in the drug. The Chinaman pays down hard lumps of sycee silver in the purchase of opium, and too often confesses, with a sigh, that he has no money to spare for cotton goods.

Few men, however, are prepared calmly and dispassionately to weigh the whole subject. In this, as in other matters, we are very liable to be misled by the cry of a party. The Archbishop of Canterbury gave wise counsel to the newly-appointed diocesan of Hong Kong, not to preach a crusade against the opium traffic.

There is just one phase of the subject which I will touch upon, namely, the opinion which the Chinese philanthropist does and must entertain of us. Some, possibly, may be disposed to sneer at this expression, Chinese *philanthropist*, and to deny his existence altogether; to set down all the protests of emperors, statesmen, and gentry as so much mere verbiage, an hypocritical appeal to principle and right, without any real meaning or purport in what they say. Much, no doubt, is mere governmental diction, old stereotyped form of words without life, though hardly without meaning; much is also anti-barbarian, a mere excuse to get rid of the hated foreigner. But all is not thus accounted for; there is real philanthropic feeling as well. How, we ask, would the head of a family in England feel towards a people who, in spite of prohibitory laws on our part, should have succeeded in introducing some most alluring vice, which had demoralized his neighbourhood, contaminated some of his own children or relatives, thrown a brother or a nephew out of a good situation, brought poverty upon a hard-working family, and multiplied the number of paupers in a parish? If we will only reason thus, we shall easily understand that the Chinese, unless we deny them the common feelings of humanity, can have had no respect for us, while their own laws were being violated, and our own implied promises were being broken; nor, even now, though the trade is legalized, can they form a high opinion of our moral probity, or consider our acquaintance desirable. As long, however, as the proprietor and tenant of the gin palace retains his place in society, so long will silent excuses, at least, be made for the large opium firms, and their agents, who sell for them the drug. Great names might be quoted in support of this opinion, but I am content to leave it on its own weight and worth. When we have stopped all the distilleries, save just enough to supply the apothecaries' shops with rum, brandy, whisky, and gin; when we have pulled down all spirit shops, and banished from respectable Christian society all distillers and wholesale or retail vendors of alcoholic liquors; then it will be time enough to talk of the iniquity of the opium trade, and the moral obliquity of all those concerned in it.

Still, we must not expect to find the quiet orderly citizen of China willing at once to receive the foreigner into his house, or to listen to the teaching of the religion which he brings. We certainly go with a very bad grace, professing our religion as one of peace and righteousness, and the blush of confusion is on our face when we are called upon, as we repeatedly are, to give a reason why we are enriching ourselves upon the misery and the vice of other people.

Our picture requires but a word of explanation. It tells graphically enough its own tale. The balls of opium which have been brought from what are still, by a merciful Providence, our Indian possessions, are being melted in the pan. The fire is lit in the small portable brick stove, on which

the pan is placed, and which is being fanned into a
red heat by the standing figure; the basket beneath
the table contains a fresh supply of charcoal; the
other pans are for still further refining. When
the opium is reduced to the consistency of thick
treacle, and is sufficiently purified of all scum, it is
fit for use. With a small bodkin, the smoker himself, or his attendant for him, takes up a little of
the treacly substance, and touches with it the
small aperture in the bowl of his pipe. He then
applies it to the flame of the lamp, and inhales the
smoke into his lungs. The figure of the opium-
smoker is a fair specimen of one who has been long
confirmed in the habit. Here is a description from
life, as I found one in the spring of the year 1855.
We were paying a visit to a small mandarin, with
whose father we were very anxious at that time
to obtain an interview. "After a while we were
ushered into an inner room, and such a scene of
poverty, filth, and degradation as there met our
eyes, it will not be easy to forget. The meanest
hovel in England could be no worse than this
miserable abode; everything was in the most di-
lapidated state. On a couch before us was the
opium pipe, with all the necessary apparatus; the
officer was just out of bed, ready for conversation,
after the effects of his pipe. We saw a man of

I

large features and of noble mien, his countenance
marked with a deep scar, which told a tale of
bravery in his country's service.   He was dressed
in miserable attire; an old and dirty handkerchief
was bound round his head; his clothes were all in
the lowest state of wretchedness."   Such is the
description which will generally apply to long-
established cases.   A greasy dress, a slouching
gait, filthy brown fingers, which have never known
the benefit of soap, a sallow countenance, and a
glazy eye, mark the victim.   Only the bloated
drunkard, with torn clothes, wild eye, and furious
demeanor, presents a more pitiable object.   May
we not express a hope that, by the labours of the
Christian philanthropist, both these may be raised
from their wretched state of degradation?

OPIUM PIPE.

No. 17.

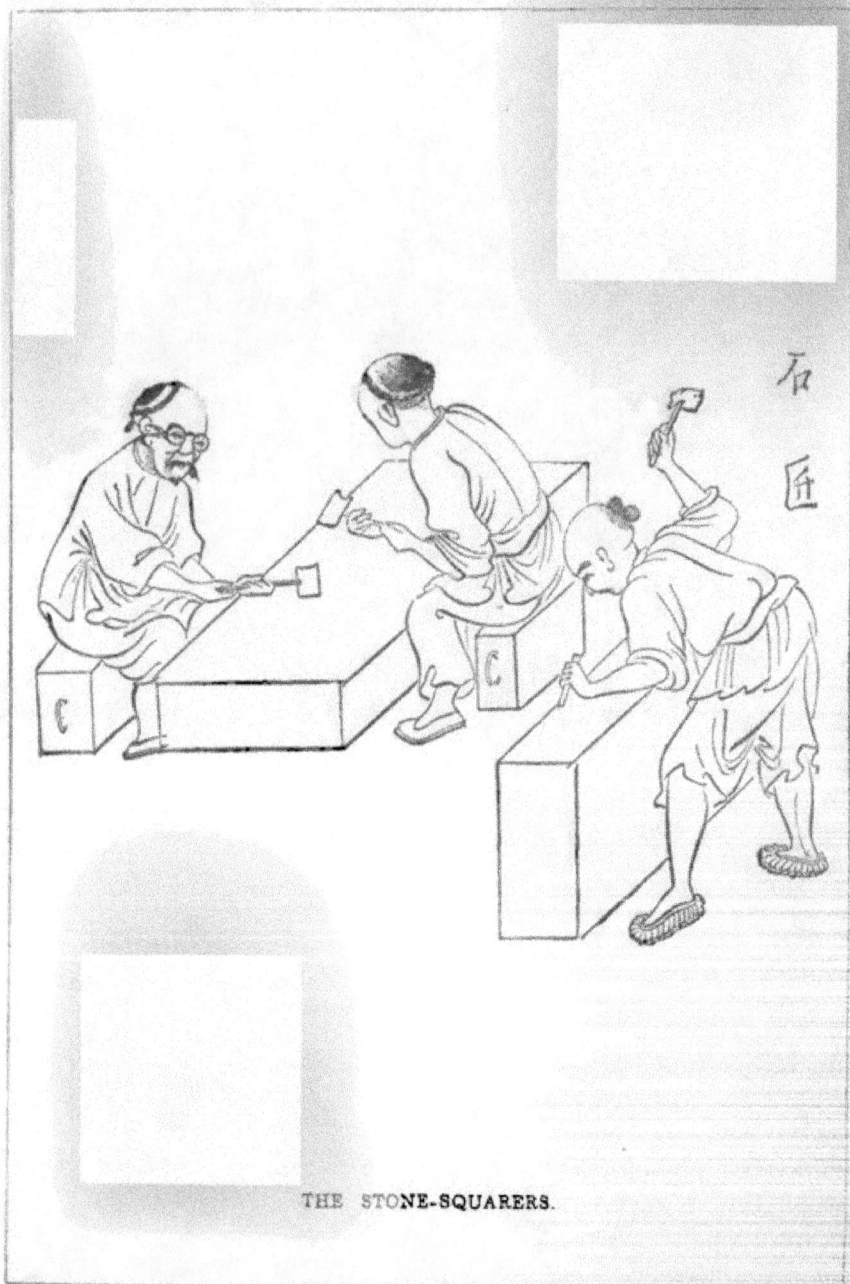

石匠

THE STONE-SQUARERS.

THE STONE-SQUARERS.

A COMMON object of interest to foreigners residing at Ningpo, is the scene of the stone quarries at Da-ying. They lie about fifteen miles to the north of the city, and may be reached either altogether by water, or partly by water and partly by land. The latter forms the more interesting journey. The canal boat will take you ten miles, easily if not swiftly, past several flourishing villages, and through some rich rice lands to a place called Do gyiao, or the Great Bridge, so named from a stone bridge of unusual height, which spans the canal just at this joint. A walk of five or six miles by the winding stone pathways, which intersect the low swampy fields, gradually leads to the foot of some bamboo or pine-clad hills. Soon the loud noise of the workmen's hammers announces the approach to the quarries. When the hills are viewed at the distance of about half a mile, the idea suggests itself that their sides have been worn or eaten away by the perpetual labour of toiling insects. This idea strikes you more forcibly as, ever and anon, some of the quarry-men are seen moving about, like tiny specs in the mouths of the caves. At the foot of the hill, just before the rugged pathway winds into its ex-cavated side, masses of stone meet the eye, which have been brought down thus far either on strong and effective barrows, or by means of poles on men's shoulders. They lie ready for the merchant, for a branch of the Ningpo river runs up to this point, and affords convenience for transport. The scene becomes more and more animated as you approach. Here men are engaged in fixing troughs in the perpendicular sides of the caves, to let off the water, which threatens to wear away the rock, and so endanger the lives of the workmen. There a knot of men is assembled, watching some huge slab yield to the force of the short iron pins driven in by laborious toil, and start from its slumber of bygone centuries. Again, in another part the regular blow of the strong hammer is heard cutting the holes into which these iron pins are to be inserted.

Let us enter one of the caves; you peep down a depth of a hundred feet, and discern a party of men at the bottom, the sound of whose voices and instruments of work echoes round the sides of the rocky shaft, and whose appearance before a large fire seems almost unearthly. Your descent, if you dare descend, is by a series of inclined planes, formed of strong poles, let in to the sides of the pit, and interlaced with hurdles of wicker work. The heel of your leather boot may now serve you in good stead, but you would feel much more comfortable if you could change shoes for a few minutes with one of the workmen. Those straw shoes or sandals, or even the calico sole of the ordinary country shoe, take a very firm hold of the ground; and though the inclined planes by which you work your zig-zag descent are very springy, and threaten to throw you off your equilibrium, yet, if you are a person of ordinary nerve, you will find no difficulty in making your way down to the bottom. Here the finest stone is found, which is the reason why this extra pains is taken to cut down towards the root of the hill. Each block of stone, as it is riven off its bed, is placed upon the barrow and wheeled up this rude staircase to the top. Many of these shafts are now filled with water; one, which was some hundred feet deep in 1848, when I first descended it, I found completely filled up about seven years afterwards. When the water rises, the workmen are compelled to beat a speedy retreat, for the appliances of force-pumps and steam-engines have not yet been adopted in China. Greater danger, however, than the rising of water is to be apprehended from the falling in of the sides of the caves. A large slip of the rock had taken place the day previous to my last visit. Fortunately the workmen had just finished their labours for the day, and were all gone home, so that no injury happened to life or limb.

Square and long blocks of various sizes are dug out from these quarries. Some are cut into elegant pillars, and carved in bold relief with dragons or other devices, to support and embellish the porticos of their temples; some form elaborate tombs and monuments of the mighty dead; some, again, are carved into grotesque figures of lions, and are annually shipped by the large native junks to Siam, to form there an ornamental entrance to the park of some grandee, which may justify the current saying, that "a rich man in Siam is known by the block of stone at his gate." Others, again, are hewn into slabs of great size (as represented in our picture), which form the sarcophagus of rich men:

others, similar to these, are for the foundation of
the houses of the wealthy, and often show a deep
moulding or ornament, which is by no means devoid
of taste in design or finish in execution. Some are
chiselled into those monuments which the nation
loves to erect in memory of the chastity and filial
devotion of its women, or the longevity of its pa-
triarchs. The more ordinary slabs pave the court-
yards of houses, or form the paths which line the
banks of rivers and canals, and divide the fields.
The refuse pieces are, if large enough, used for
rough stone walls or the foundations of houses; if
too small for any useful purpose, they are cast aside,
and gradually form a bank forty or fifty feet high,
by the side of the quarry's mouth. The work is
usually executed in a rude way on the spot. When
a purchase is made, the rude blocks are taken away,
and more carefully wrought up in the stonemason's
yard. The right-hand figure of our etching shows
a workman engaged in cutting off with a strong
chisel some roughnesses in the stone. The two other
figures, each sitting upon his box of tools for want
of a better seat (a very common feature in Chinese
economy), are each of them armed with a thick and
heavy iron mallet-head, attached to a pliant handle
of very tough wood. With this they lightly and

rapidly tap the plane surface of the stone till it becomes smooth enough for use.

The spectacles of the elder figure belong rather to the individual than to his work; for though doubtless many an accident to the eyes would be saved by their adoption, yet, in this as in other trades, men are usually reckless. Steel filers and others will not avail themselves of those means which science has discovered and provided for the prevention of dangers to which their calling exposes them.

The reader has doubtless noticed the head-dress of these as well as of other artizans throughout our book. The two workmen engaged in smoothing the surface of the stone block have only thought it necessary to wind their queues round the top of their head, and so keep them out of harm's way, and prevent their being soiled by the dust which their employment creates. The other, a more ordinary workman, whose toil is rougher and more laborious, has gathered his hair into a peculiar double knot, which he fastens with a smooth short pin of bamboo. Before he mixes with the world around, he must engage either a barber, or the friendly hand of wife, daughter, or mother to unloose the unsightly knot, and braid the long hair

into its customary plait. The other two men have
only to unwind their queues, and then, with the
addition of a long robe, they are fit for the society
of their fellows. These artizans are by no means
deficient in talent. If we may judge by the mas-
sive bridges which cross the rivers or arms of the
sea, by the temples and private houses which have
been built throughout the country, and by those
monuments carved in the boldest *bas-relief*, with
figures of men and animals, which are deservedly
the admiration of foreigners, we must say of the
Chinese stone-cutters that they are not behind the
rest of their countrymen, and make good their
claim to a high grade in the rank of artizans.

TEA CUPS.

TEMPLE OF THE HEAVENLY WINDS.

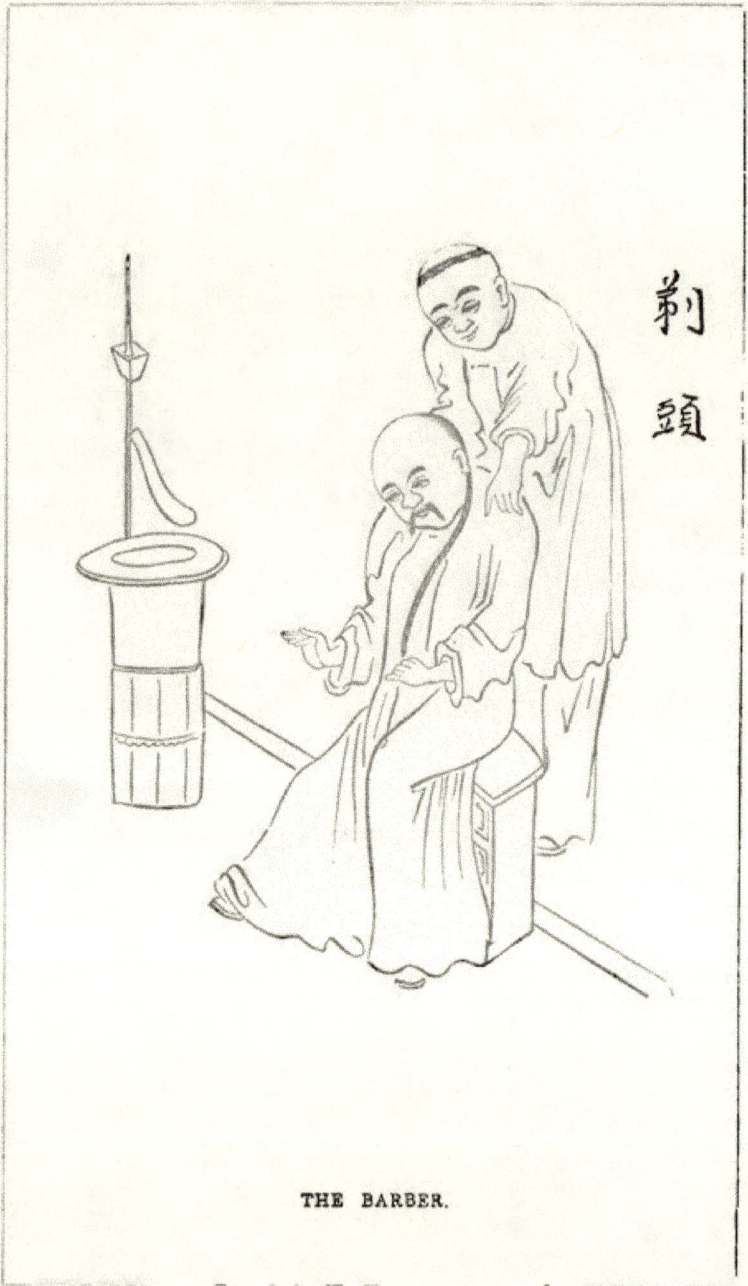

剃
頭

THE BARBER.

THE BARBER.

OUR great authority in razors, razor-strops, and all connected with the *civilized* art of shaving, tells us, that "the great secret of easy shaving is the thorough softening of the beard with water before commencing the operation." From cases of casual personal experience, I fear that the "secret" is not yet divulged to the public, or that, if divulged, they are not yet satisfied of its utility. I may, however, add my mite to Mr. Mechi's assertion, by the mention of the fact that a nation of 180 millions of *men*, not including their Tartar conquerors, from whom they derived the custom, manage, without any pain or inconvenience, to take off all the hair on their heads, which is notorious for its coarseness, by the simple action of the razor, without any other preparatory process than that of thoroughly softening it with the hottest endurable water. While our young shavers find it difficult

with all their Naples soap, wonderful creams, half-
guinea razors, Mechi strops, et cetera, to get rid of
the little more than downy covering of their skins,
the coarse, thick, black stumps of Tartar and
Chinese heads yield, *without the use of any soap*, to the
action of a little bit of hardened iron, two inches
long by an inch wide. I do not mean to deny the
advantage of a little good lather in keeping moist
the beard which has previously been well softened,
and in assisting the passage of the razor over the
face; but the chief advantage does not lie here. It
no doubt looks pretty to cover the face with a
creamy surface, and many a young gentleman ad-
mires every morning his snow-white upper lip and
chin; it is also interesting to watch how this yields
to the razor's stroke, so that you can tell to an
inch what part has been gone over; but how often
does the soap only come away, while the refractory
beard is left, and the razor gets the blame which it
does not deserve. Let Mr. Mechi's words be heard,
and let the 200 and odd millions of Chinese and
Tartars join in the cry, till the "secret" is really
out, believed in, and acted upon, and the face gets
a good plunging and sousing before the edge of the
steel is applied.

Although the barbers' shops are not, as with us,

distinguished by the pole and bandage, yet they
seem to show that the barber originally knew something of the healing art; for you now constantly
see, in passing their open front, the operation of
shampooing performed previous to shaving. I
retain quite fresh to the present day the impress of
the first case which I witnessed. A sallow Chinaman, stretched at full length on an easy chair, had
surrendered himself entirely to the tender mercies
of the manipulator, who, sitting by his side, was
pommelling him all over his body, but chiefly on
the legs and chest, with partially-closed fists. I
have regretted since that I never submitted to the
operation, so as to be able to prove or disprove the
truth of the assertion, that a delightful sensation
was the result of all this tapping.

About three cash, or half a farthing, is the usual
sum demanded for simply shaving the head. If the
queue is plaited and interwoven with fresh silk, the
scale of charges rises accordingly. A good razor costs
about two-pence; the best strop, consisting of a
strip of peculiarly-made stout calico, brought from
some distance in the interior of the country, may
be had for one penny; thus it does not cost very
much to furnish a barber's shop. The chief item of
expense is the metal basin, made of a kind of brass,

which is kept beautifully bright and clean. No Chinaman is his own barber; indeed, as the top of the head is usually the only part which requires touching, (for the beard of the Chinese does not often give him much trouble,) it would be at too great a risk of self-destruction to hazard the attempt with one's own hand. This of course gives employment to a vast number of persons. It is said that, in Canton, there are between seven and eight thousand of the barber's calling; and by a calculation roughly made of the number shaved by each "hand," I should think this a correct estimate. Shaving, and braiding the queue, fastening a new tail to a worn-out stump, and shampooing, are the only arts required of the barber. False moustache and beards of a rude kind, as worn by actors in the public shows, are not made by his hands; and he has yet to be initiated into the European art of making perukes for the votaries of fashion.

Since the incoming of the Manchow power, barbers' shops must have undergone a considerable change; for the native Chinese, till they received this badge of a foreign yoke, did not allow either knife or scissors to pass upon their head, but were the "long-haired" race, which the present insurgents, the followers of Tai ping, are wishing to become. They are naturally anxious to do away with this mark of subjection to their Tartar conquerors, and recur to the ancient fashion, which was to bind the long hair in a knot on the top of their head, and to fasten it through with a wooden or metal pin, as is often represented in the old pictures of the Ming dynasty.

Those who affirm that shaving debilitates and makes degenerate a people, have here rather a large bolus of objection to swallow. The Tartars shave, and yet conquer the unshorn Chinamen; the China-men, compulsorily shorn, are now threatening to subvert again the power of their Tartar conquerors. Verily some other power besides the razor is at work here!

The Chinese gentleman is not so particular about his head as the English gentleman is about his beard. Where the latter shaves at all, he shaves daily; it may be, if he dines or spends the evening away from home, twice a-day. The former on an average lets his head be three days without being touched. Our servants were content with once a week. Saturday night always saw them with shin-ing polls, ready for the Sunday services. School boys were served in the same way. Ordinary la-bourers, left to their own resources, will often wait from five to ten days, sometimes even more; but after that time the head looks very unsightly, and formidable with upstanding bristles half an inch long.

In the case of mourning, the law, or rather the recognized custom, more powerful than law, is to keep the head unshaven for so many months, in proportion to the nearness of relationship to the party deceased. The thirteen months' absence of tonsure for either of one's parents, if strictly observed, would show a shock of hair too frightful for ordinary society to endure; so that, where strict attention to the laws of etiquette forbids the clean polish of the razor's blade, other means are employed to keep the stumps of the hair within due bounds.

As to barbers' shops, customs vary in different parts of the country. Thus, in the accounts given us of the south, we are told that "the barbers are all ambulatory; each carries his shop on his back, and performs his operations tonsorial in the open street." In the north this rule is reversed. All the barbers have shops, which (like other shops) are open to the street, but are unlike only in this, that they are without counters. They are usually ornamented with hanging scrolls, often caricatures of foreigners and their habits. They are furnished with easy chairs and small basin-stands, similar to that represented in the engraving. If the weather be hot, the chair or stool is placed just outside the threshold of the house, and the operation of shaving, &c., goes on in the open street. The Chinaman has no such squeamishness about these things as we have, and is surprised that we get angry (as some of us do) when, in our excursions into the interior, rude hands pull off the covering of the travelling boat, and a gaping crowd persists in seeing the morning ablutions.

The art of hair-cutting, as practised in the West, is as yet unknown to the Chinese barber. It is not often, therefore, that the foreigner calls in the aid of native skill; only when he assumes the garb of the country, does he find this necessary. Admirably effected is this finishing stroke to the foreigner's transformation. The queue fastened on to the back hair deceives even the practised eye of the native; and, as Mr. Fortune quaintly says, the dogs even take no notice, and let you pass unchallenged.

No barber's art is required for the women's hair, no shops are set apart for their use; they are invariably their own hair-dressers. In the case of the wealthy, private apartments conceal the operation

K

from casual observance; in that of the poorer classes, every street in the forenoon gives you an opportunity of witnessing this part of the women's toilet. It is no summary process, and whether gazed upon or not, they proceed very leisurely with their work. An English lady who had had plenty of opportunity of knowing, assured me that the China woman spends a good hour of her everyday life in the performance of this one portion of her toilet.

A CHINESE RAIN-CLOAK.

桃
水

THE WATER-CARRIERS.

THE WATER-CARRIERS.

THE Chinaman of the rice plains depends upon the heavens for his supply of drinking-water. Even in the hill country, where the streams are comparatively pure, rain-water, or as he calls it, "sky-water," holds the first place in his estimation. The water of wells is in all cases avoided, because of the medicinal properties inseparable from it. Science has taught us that his estimate of the purity of these different waters is correct; and we should not have to complain so often of bad tea, did we but follow his example, and line the backs of our houses with a row of huge earthenware jars, or what is better still, in building a house, arrange for the construction of a large tank, which should receive the showers and dews of heaven. Of course I do not here speak of London or the smoky precincts of our manufacturing cities. Droughts, however, frequently take place, when the supply of rain-water in the dwellings of the middle classes is exhausted. Only a few of the more wealthy families have furnished their court-yards with a number of these jars, sufficient to enable them to hold out till the supply comes. In this case, if we may continue to use the proverb in its perverted meaning, the ill-wind blows some good to the water-carriers, who undertake, from a neighbouring pool or the river's side, to supply the different householders. An animated scene then daily takes place. In the thorough-fares men are continually passing and repassing, laden with their heavy burden: their painful toil is, however, lightened to them by the consideration that they are earning at least double their ordinary wages. The picture presents a scene very familiar to myself; it is no doubt taken from a central spot for drawing water, which overhangs a narrow neck of the large intramural lake, in the city of Ningpo. In every season of drought this is the constant resort of the water-carrier, who drives a brisk trade by filling the water-butts of large houses in the adjacent streets. In the families of the poor, recourse is had to the well, but only when all other resources fail. The alluvial plain on which the city of Ningpo is situated, yields only water which is both unpleasant to the palate, and unwholesome to the stomach.

Foreigners very frequently suffer great inconvenience from the badness of the water in the wells, and the scanty supply of that in the water jars. When rain-water fails, they are compelled either to depend upon these hard-working coolies, and to drink the water—such as it is—drawn from this lake; or they are driven to the expedient of sending a water-boat some twenty miles up the country, to bring down from the mountain streams a sufficient quantity to replenish their exhausted tanks. A curious sight these boats present. Laden to the very water's edge with their precious cargo, they seem in imminent danger of foundering : the wave of the smallest tug-boat on our rivers would swamp them in an instant.

This inconvenience does not press so heavily upon the Chinaman as upon the foreigner. A comparatively small amount of water satisfies him. He never scrubs his floors; for his ablutions, he is content with just as much scalding water as will cover the bottom of a flat brass basin. In this he lays a coarse cotton napkin, with which he spunges his face and hands. In respectable families, this process is repeated after the principal

meal of the day. Even in the public baths, the
shallow stone-cistern for washing has only two or
three inches depth of water, and this is shared in
common by five or ten persons. The stench, as
may be supposed, is insufferably bad. No Chinaman thinks of washing the whole body more than
once a year. On this occasion, the dogs also, by
immemorial custom, share in the privilege.

There is also another reason why the Chinaman
does not feel the absence of those deep and cold
wells which are so much prized by us, and which
we so much miss in his land; he not only abhors
the touch, but also the taste, of cold water. He
never takes a draught of man's original beverage.
Tea of some kind, *i. e.* boiled water, generally with
some herb infused, is his drink. I have frequently
found on my journeys, that a look of incredulity,
an expression of surprise, and a close scrutiny of
the glass, always followed the act of my drinking
off a tumbler of cold water. Only the evidence
of their senses convinced the bystanders that I
was not drinking alcohol.

The hard-working coolie will always find this
tea which he loves at the resting-places, built at
intervals of a few miles on most of the main roads.
They are the work of wealthy individuals, who have

left the funds for the perpetual support of such an institution. These persons deserve the thanks of their countrymen, and the praise of all who desire to promote the welfare of the poor man. Would that our people were thus supplied with an innocuous draught, and so saved the necessity of spending their hard-earned money by deep potations of medicated beer, merely for the sake of quenching thirst, at the alehouse. Happily a beginning has lately been made, which seems likely to spread far and wide through our land. Plain water suits us better than lukewarm tea; from our deep wells it will always flow up cold and pure, and there is hardly a neighbourhood in the vicinity of large towns, which would not be much benefited by a common pump and conveniences for drinking. It is one of the happiest suggestions of our day, and deserves the support of all who are interested in the condition of the poorer classes. No man is deprived by this means of his lawful gratification; the mug of beer, if desired, is as accessible as before; no American or Caledonian law forbids; the great advantage is, that a man is not driven to strong drink merely for the sake of assuaging thirst.

WATER-WHEEL FOR IRRIGATION.

THE PHYSIOGNOMIST.

No. 20.

THE PHYSIOGNOMIST.

IT was no novel theory which the great Lavater propounded to the world. He did not pretend to have discovered, but only sought to develope and establish an ancient branch of science. At a very remote age, physiognomy was known and studied in India, that great cradle of our western civilization; while Pythagoras seems to have met with it in Egypt, and to have imported it thence, and taught it to his own countrymen. In China, too, from time immemorial, the sides of the streets have been occupied by stalls similar to that in our engraving; where a doctor of the science strokes his thin moustache, and invites the passer-by to make trial of his skill.

Physiognomy, however, has never taken the place which was expected by its advocates among the exact sciences. Lavater's unqualified belief in it, and admiration of it, is placed by most among the other eccentricities of the good dean. He maintains that it can be reduced to rule, communicated and taught. He declares that it was to him a source of pure mental gratification; that it afforded him a new view of the perfection of Deity, and displayed a new scene of harmony and beauty in his works.

While, however, men hold aloof from all those conclusions to which minds like Lavater's have come on the subject, they yet seldom fail to make practical use of the science in the ordinary business of life. What merchant, for example, does not narrowly scrutinize the features of the clerk whom he is about to place in a confidential situation? What brother, on hearing that his sister is to be given away in marriage, does not at once endeavour to read the soul of the man in the mould and expression of his features? Singularly accurate, too, is the estimate which one man is often able to form of another at the very first glance. Nor should we be surprised at this; for when Lavater saw the character of each donor engraven on the hand which dropped his gift into the velvet almsbag in the church of Zurich; and when the single feature of the nose has been gravely maintained to constitute a type of individuality, we might reasonably expect that the whole countenance, with its

differences of feature, outline, and expression, would
be considered a correct indication of natural disposition.

In our engraving we see a professor of this art,
one who evidently has no mean opinion of himself,
or of the science which he represents. The large
single face is supposed to be a perfect specimen of
the human countenance. It answers to the care-
fully-marked heads in the studio of the phrenologist. By its standard of excellence the consulting
party will be scrutinized and judged. Some particulars, also, of his future history will be indis-
tinctly mapped out; for the science is in China
debased by its connection with fortune-telling and
astrology. One peculiarity in the art of Chinese
physiognomy is the supposed type which belongs to
four classes—the poor, the rich, the noble, and the
mean. They are represented in the four heads on
the wall of the room, beginning at the left hand,
which is the poor man. The second figure of
the *rich* man reminds us that money, among its
other uses, has been freely employed in the purchase of fat pork, prime poultry, luscious turtle,
and other rich esculents, which may have given to
his face that peculiar roundness which belongs to
it. The peacock's feather of the third adds no

little to his appearance of nobility. There is no difficulty in recognizing the mean and ignoble stamp of the fourth figure.

There are also other marks which guide the physiognomist in the exercise of his art. The two friends who were associated with me had each his own characteristic, which the Chinaman envied. In one, this feature was length of ears; in the other, a round contour of face. The former was considered the mark of talent, the latter (as has been said), that of riches. For myself, the length and straightness of my nose most frequently drew attention; but this, I imagine, was more from its contrast with their own peculiar *thick snubs*, than because of any particular virtue which belonged to this feature.

If the science of physiognomy had not been so intimately connected with astrology, so much discredit would not have been thrown upon it. It is chiefly on this account, as well as from the uncertainty which attends its application, that men not only refuse to accredit it as a science, but even ridicule it as a folly. M. Formey, indeed, argues that the human frame may by sickness or other accidents undergo considerable changes, without any correspondent change of disposition; so that although the science itself might be founded on truth, the right exercise of it might baffle all human powers of perception. Others, again, have observed that natural passions may remain strongly marked in the features, while they have been subdued by severe mental effort, thus causing the face to be no true index of the mind. We are reminded here of the anecdote of Socrates, whose character, as read by the physiognomists of his time in the lines of his face, totally differed from that which his every-day life was exhibiting among his fellow citizens. The story runs, that on being called to the market-place to have his face examined by the physiognomist practising there, he was pronounced passionate, sensual, and intemperate. When a roar of vulgar laughter greeted this assertion, Socrates quietly said that Zopyrus had read him aright, and explained the apparent failure of the man of science, by saying that in natural disposition he was such as had been described, but that he had overcome by severe discipline those vices which threatened to domineer over him. It is well known also that Napoleon himself, no mean judge of character, came to the conclusion that "no reliance whatever was to be placed on the expression of the face."

Even the science of phrenology, which seems less open to objection—inasmuch as no hypocrisy, however subtle, could change the formation of the skull—is, after all, from more causes than one, but an imperfect guide. The same thing may happen which we have supposed possible in physiognomy, and the natural temperament, represented correctly in the formation of the skull, may have been much altered by external or mental influences. All men, however, are practically physiognomists. We usually judge of a new acquaintance by his face, and form a favourable or unfavourable opinion of him at the very first glance; while such expressions as these—"Nobility is stamped on his very looks," "He has the face of a scoundrel," "Such a benevolent expression!" "Such a morose cast of countenance!"—are familiar to all. Their use proves that persons are—it may be unconsciously to themselves—in the constant exercise of this art; and we know that in some instances they show a remarkable aptitude in its right application. Let any one examine the plates in Lavater's work, and he will find himself pronouncing a definite and, in the main, a correct judgment on each form there delineated. Probably the most untutored savage could not go into the "chamber of horrors" in the waxwork exhibition in Baker Street—where Rush, Greenacre, and a hundred other notorieties figure —without an instinctive sensation that he was looking at villains.

The old proverb, " Fronti nulla fides," is most useful as a caution in a world where so much hypocrisy attempts to veil the truth; yet an open and ingenuous look will always make a favourable impression, and, in the great majority of cases, will not deceive.

A TRADING JUNK.

A MOUNTAIN CHAIR.

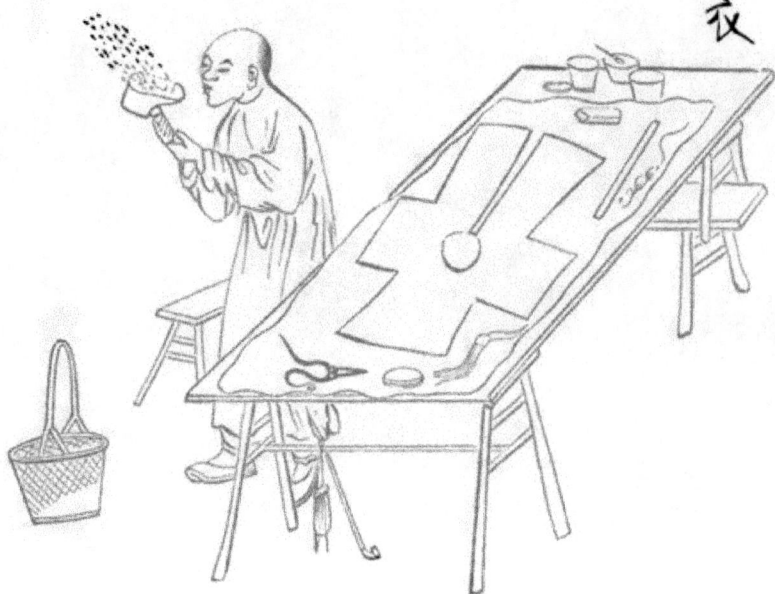

成衣

THE TAILOR.

THE TAILOR.

IT is a common saying in China that "the tailor
is the greatest sinner in the world." No sooner
(say they) has a piece of stuff been finished with
infinite toil and industry, than he proceeds to cut
it with his huge scissors into unsightly pieces.

There are many peculiarities about the Chinese
tailor, which make him differ from his European
brother; and even where the implements of his
trade are the same in kind, they are often very
different in appearance. Some of these peculiarities are not a little amusing. First of all, he never
uses the measuring tape. Instead of trying the
arm at the shoulder, the elbow, the wrist; the leg
at the hip, the knee, the ankle; the width across
the shoulders, the girth of the body, the length
of the waist, he does all this either at a glance,—
and then the slight movement of the lips seems
to be saying, Hem! two inches taller than I am,
a little stouter, rather long arms, a thick neck,—

L

or at most the foot-rule, in carpenter-like style, is run over the person, and a measurement sufficiently accurate is thus obtained. There is then a regular proportion for each piece; and a chalked line, similar to, though much smaller than that used by our carpenters, is employed to mark out the shape. This line is seen in our picture lying on the table, attached to the little bag filled with chalk dust, through which it passes. When the scissors, following the white mark of the chalked cord, have done their work of cutting the material into pieces of the proper number and shape, the next process is that which answers to our basting. The word, however, is spelt with a p instead of a b, that is to say, the Chinese tailor, instead of lightly stitching down his pieces, preparatory to sewing, fastens their edges by means of a strong paste. In other words, he pastes instead of bastes his work. If the reader has ever received any raised figures on calico, silk, or satin, from the flowery land, he will probably have observed their tendency to mould and decay; the simple reason being, that the paste employed in place of stitching has never become thoroughly dry, or that the damp of the sea voyage has caused it to become moist, and the garments have literally fallen to

pieces, as if smitten by leprosy: here a richly-
wrought shoe, and there an embroidered skirt, here
a part of the head dress, and there an ornamental
cuff, has peeled off, and left a mutilated and unsightly figure. This pot of paste, with the tiny
spatula used in its application, are shown in our
picture at one end of the table. Clothes thus
cut and fashioned might naturally be supposed
to assume the form of a mere shapeless sack on
the Chinaman's person, and the tailor's art be
reduced apparently to very simple and rude operations, but it is not so. The true artist, even in
China, discovers his ability; and good tailors, earning twice the wages of less-gifted ones, are in as
much demand in China as in Europe. In stitching, we have the decided superiority; in fact the
palm is yielded to us, even by the Chinese tailor.
I have often heard members of the craft confess
that they learned much, during our occupation of
Chusan, by examining the uniforms of our troops
and the plain clothes of our officers, which showed,
even to their eyes, a far higher character of workmanship.

The Chinaman's habit of doing everything
differently from ourselves, evinced in numberless
instances of greater or less moment, and more

or less ludicrous, is seen here too, even in the
manner of his sewing. The Chinese tailor does
not sew *to* him, but *from* him, pushing the needle
through the garment with a broad ring fastened
on his thumb.

I must beg the reader to notice that curious
instrument, from which a cloud of dust is issuing,
as with a strong puff the tailor blows it from him.
Behold the goose of the Chinese tailor, or in plain
English the ironing-box, which is nothing more
than a horse-shoe-shaped saucepan, without a lid,
filled with live charcoal, and thus kept hot for
hours together. This same dust, arising from the
impalpable ashes of the charcoal, blown about the
room is a great nuisance, and is very repugnant to
our notions of cleanliness.

The tailor's board is worthy of observation. It
is nearly always extemporized for the occasion,
usually consisting of a wide door taken off its
hinges, set upon two high stools, and covered
with a drab felt cloth. Here the strong common
sense of our Chinese friends is shown. They *sit* at
their board, as at a table, to work, and so are saved
from those diseases to which our sons of the
needle are exposed from their stooping and cramped
posture.

The foot-measure, formed of a slip of bamboo, divided into ten parts, is somewhat longer than our own, and exceeds by about two inches the foot-rule used in carpenters' and masons' work. The pipe, never long absent from the Chinaman's lips, is seen under the table, ready for use. The little leather purse contains the tobacco, while a small case, not shown in the picture, is furnished with flint, steel, and tinder. The lucifer-match is a convenience unknown to the Chinese, or at least but very lately and very sparsely introduced. These scissors, which in our hands would prove a very clumsy instrument, deserve notice from their quaint, snake-like form. Strange and awkward as their shape appears, they are yet made to do their work well in the skilful hand of the initiated.

The wages of the tailor we were surprised to find lower than those of almost every other trade, an inferiority of remuneration which he owes to his own dishonest practices. Abstraction of the stuffs committed to his charge by his customers is his incurable vice, against which they on their part protect themselves by the lowness of the wages paid for his work; and thus his notorious dishonesty has introduced a nefarious system, in which theft of his customer's property supplements the low remuneration which he obtains. One case, and one only, has come under my own observation, where, after years had passed away, Christian conscientiousness led to the desire to restore that which common custom had permitted to be taken, and restoration was in fact made, to the great surprise of the person to whom it was offered.

The thread used, even for ordinary work, is of silk. Cotton thread is rarely seen; it figures as a curiosity in the shop-fronts of the smaller linendrapers.

The women's dresses, save among the poor, are invariably made by men. The richer and more delicate embroidery is also done by their hands: and when some of the ladies of our small foreign community needed satin bonnets, and did not care to go to the expense of the home article, or to wait the delay of the order and the five months' voyage, a tailor was called in, who, with that versatility of talent which is so characteristic of the people, soon followed the foreign "muster" (Anglicè, pattern), and fitted them to admiration.

One feature of Chinese tailoring distinct from our own is the absence of those large establishments which we call "tailors." No one goes to a tailor's to order a garment, but purchases his own

material at the shop, and then sends for a working-
hand, who comes to his house at so much per day.
Those large handsome shops, such as we find in
the metropolis or in our principal provincial towns,
whose masters are in some instances the owners of
princely estates, and who by the influence derived
from wealth occupy a high position in society, are
entirely absent from Chinese cities.

As in my sketch of the cobbler, I took the opportunity of saying something about Chinese shoes,
so would I avail myself of the sketch of the tailor,
to say a word or two on Chinese dress. No nation
pays greater attention to this matter, or is more
particular about the adaptation of the material,
both as to quality and quantity, to the season.
Our inattention to it is, to an unbiassed observer,
simply ludicrous. In all our three great professions, the same material prevails for coat, waistcoat,
and trousers, whatever be the season. In some of
our campaigns in hot climates, the thick coat and
heavy hat have destroyed more lives than the sword
and bullet of the enemy.* The only answer to

---

* Hundreds of letters might be quoted, written during the late
war in India, all concurring in this testimony. Thus, in a letter from
Allahabad, dated June 28th, the writer says: " It is wretched to see

those who urge objections against the black cloth
coat and stiff hat on an oppressive summer's day,
is a groan against the exactions of polite society.
Things are mending among us, but we have much
yet to accomplish. Mark now the Chinaman. His
material is changed with the changing season.
He has every variety of texture, from the stout
broad cloths of Russia and England, fur-lined,
thickly-wadded overcoats, down to the flimsiest
silk gauze or grass-cloth which the loom can spin.
In the depth of winter, when the thermometer
stands often some ten degrees below freezing point,
no fire is used; indeed, except in the kitchen, the
houses are not provided with fire-places, nor are
any stoves used beyond a small charcoal pan for
the feet. The only way, therefore, by which to
fence off the cold is to put on extra clothing,
which is done to a degree which quite surprises

how the soldiers die, particularly on the march, from sun-stroke and
apoplexy. Hundreds who have died might have been saved,—in
fact, never would have been taken ill at all,—if the Government
would only give the men a decent protection for the head, instead
of the wretched little forage cap, which is no protection at all.
When I was in the Bays, out of a detachment of about 300 men, in
a fortnight we buried twenty-two men and one officer, every one of
them from sun-stroke and apoplexy. Many regiments have been
losing men at the rate of half a dozen per diem."

us. Those only who have amused themselves with
skipning an onion can have any idea of the number
of garments which are successively stripped from a
Chinaman's back in the winter season. The long
wadded or fur-lined robe which completes the
Chinaman's suit, buttons close round the neck,
reaches down nearly to the feet, and envelopes the
whole body. It is an admirable invention, and one
most suited to the quiet habits and sedate walk of
the Asiatic gentry. Not that we could make any
general use of it, any more than we could endure the
long finger-nails of the Eastern scholar. Amongst
ourselves it could only be suited for the dressing-
room, into which its merits may ere long gain for
it an introduction. A late advertisement, "The
dressing-dress, an Eastern suggestion," made one
think whether, among our new fashions, we might
not soon have something very like the long warm
robe of our Chinese friends.

Altogether China stands high in the matter of
dress. She will not suffer, either in the material
of her fabrics, or the shape of her clothes, or the
workmanship of her artizans, in comparison with
most other nations. In some respects she has the
decided superiority; and if we take into conside-

ration the nature of the climate, and the character of the people, with the exception of the women's bandaged feet, we shall find it difficult to criticise the suitableness or the efficiency of any portion of the male or female attire.

A SPORTSMAN.

挑糞

THE SCAVENGER.—No. 1.

THE SCAVENGER.

NOTHING can well be more graphic than this phase of Chinese life. My friend, the artist, doubtless felt that I had a difficult subject to handle, so he has given me one of his most pleasing and life-like etchings. I would gladly have avoided a subject like this, had I not felt that my pictures of Chinese life would be incomplete without it. No foreigner has lived long among the native community without carrying away with him vivid recollections of these scavengers; and, wherever he has summoned up courage to speak on the subject, his information has invariably been followed with an exclamation of astonishment. It is a matter difficult to handle without being offensive to squeamish minds. The *Times'* correspondent, in his most graphic letters, was almost the first who boldly and plainly spoke out, but it is, nevertheless, one of vast social importance. Those who remember how Father Thames became, in the drought of last summer, fetid with decomposed matter, threatening the lives of thousands compelled to live in its vicinity, and forcing attention upon statesmen of both Houses of Parliament, may be disposed to listen for a few minutes to what I have to say on the main drainage of large Chinese cities.

Here, I trust, all who are afraid of a practical subject, which deals with gross matters of detail, will shut their eyes, and turn over two or three leaves, when they will find something more to their taste. Having thus given fair warning, I may proceed.

Be it known, then, that in Chinese cities and towns no underground sewers or drains exist, save a rudely-constructed covered gutter in the centre of the larger streets, which carries off the superfluous rain and the few slops of the houses lining the wayside. The rivers or canals, therefore, which lie in the outskirts of large towns, or even upon which large cities are situated, are comparatively pure. A bather in the stream, above or below the city, would find little or no difference in the purity of the water, which is measured rather by the number of boats plying upon its surface, than by the population inhabiting its banks.

Rows of large earthen jars, each standing about three feet high by three in diameter,—or an im-

mense tank, built of slabs of stone carefully
cemented together,—are sunk by the sides of
thronged thoroughfares, even in the midst of
towns or cities; over these are built wooden
sheds, open towards the road: no attempt at
concealment by boarding or doors in front being
made. To the European this gives the appearance
of gross indecency, though, by the force of habit, it
is not considered in the slightest degree to offend
against the laws of propriety. As, then, either
these public receptacles, or similar ones in private
dwellings, become full, the scavenger of our picture
comes and takes away the contents in his large
pails, which he carries, as usual, by a stout pole, or
split bamboo, across his shoulders. If a canal is
in the neighbourhood, he provides, at a convenient
spot, a large empty boat, into which the contents
of his pails are discharged. It is thus moved off
into the country, and sold to the farmers and occu-
piers of the land, who store it in similar earthen
jars, which they keep at the corners of their fields,
where the foot-paths intersect, ready for use. Woe
to the unfortunate traveller who brings his boat to
an anchor, after a weary day's journey, just under
the lee of one of these vessels of perfumery, as
it has often happened to myself, when I invariably

found the boatmen unable to sympathize with my strong feelings of annoyance; and who, if other arguments failed, would try to comfort me as the Taoutai of Shanghai comforted Her Majesty's consul, who complained of the stench of a public convenience immediately under the walls of his (then) Chinese residence, by saying that it was very wholesome.*

It is said that "the Chinese mix their night-soil with one-third of its weight of fat marl, make it into cakes, and dry it by exposure to the sun. In this state it is free from any disagreeable smell, and forms a common article of commerce in the empire."

This may be true in some parts of the country, but I have never seen it, nor heard of it, during my residence in China.

As to the absence of smell, I doubt if this advantage would appear so great to a Chinaman as

* In an excursion made to the monastery of Teen-tung in the year 1845, by Mr., now Dr. Smith, Bishop of Victoria, he says, "Instead of the fresh breezes of autumn, and the inhalations of the pure country air, the rice-fields and gardens gave forth most offensive odours, caused by the manure with which the ripening crops were covered. Not a particle of refuse is lost by this people, who place large jars and vessels in every corner of their villages to receive these seeds of fertility and wealth. Boats passed and repassed laden with this disagreeable cargo."

it would to one of ourselves; his olfactory organs are decidedly much less sensitive than our own. I also doubt whether the absence of smell would not imply absence of fertilizing power and strength. So it has been proved in our large towns where the deodorizing process has been employed; the fertilizing property has evaporated, and its value, as a manure, has been so greatly deteriorated as to be hardly worth even the cost of cartage to the land. The names of night-men and night-soil, which we have given as euphemisms to this occupation and commodity, are inapplicable in China, for all its collecting and removal, as well as application, is carried on in open day. There are few things more offensive to the foreign inhabitant of a Chinese city, during the summer-months especially, than the presence, in the very narrow and crowded streets, of men similar to our picture. We stumble upon them at every turn, and no little caution is needed to avoid the calamity of contact. Occasionally, also, through a slip of the foot, or the giving way of the carrying gear, the contents of the pails is upset and floods the foot-path. Not very long since, the city of Hangchow, which numbers about a million of inhabitants, was put to very serious inconvenience by a rupture between these

men, who form a separate class, and a mandarin.
It appears that one of them had inadvertently run
against the great man's sedan-chair, who, in his
annoyance, ordered him to be bastinadoed. All
his fraternity took up his cause, and when the
sentence of the magistrate was carried into effect,
they, to a man, refused to do any more work till
an apology was made. So determined were they,
and so high did the feud run, that the city was
brought to the point of suffocation, and the mandarin was obliged to yield the point, so far offering
an apology as to acknowledge that he had been too
hasty, and that the punishment of the offender was
unjust. Hangchow, but for this reparation, exacted
by the offended majesty of the scavengers, might
have been dug out from under a heap of human
guano ; but concession restored it to its former
condition of prosperity, and it still exists to tell
the tale of the ruin which once impended it.

The manure is used for almost all the *vegetable*
crops. The rice lands are flooded in the early
spring, and some deposit is thus obtained to enrich
and renovate the soil. They are also sown with a
clover-layer, which is ploughed into the land. Bul-
locks and horses are so few in number, in comparison with the population, that long manure is hardly

換糞

an appreciable fraction of the whole. All the tribe
of vegetables and plants which require to be rapidly
developed, such as cabbages, beans, cucumbers,
melons, Indian corn, millet, and some of the
choicer flowers, are treated with this manure in a
liquid state. The instrument used for this purpose (which is shown in the sketch opposite) is
simply a small spouted tub, fixed to the end of a
pole. The manure is then poured over the plant,
and left to find its way to the roots. This process
ceases some weeks before the vegetables are cut for
the market; a very necessary fact to be known,
but one which, even when known, hardly reconciles
the foreigner to the sight of Chinese greens on his
dinner-table. It is generally allowed that an ex-
cessive quantity of manure imparts a strong and
disagreeable flavour to vegetables, and this is found
to be the case with those cultivated in the Chinese
gardens.

The whole subject is one which may well occupy
the attention of English agriculturists. In no
matter of practical farming are we so deficient as
in this. Holland, and other continental nations,
are very far in advance of us. It is only of late
years that much attention has been paid to the
subject. Many schemes have been proposed for

M

making effective the sewerage of our large cities, and especially of the metropolis; but none has as yet been brought forward which has carried conviction of its feasibility. We could not, indeed, adopt the almost primitive plan of the Chinese; still, stone or cemented cess-pools, which should receive the drainage both of houses and stables, might, by degrees, be introduced into every well-regulated establishment, and be essential to the plan of any stables or sheds for horses and cattle.

It is calculated that from the city of London alone there falls into the Thames a million pounds sterling per annum, and when we add to this statement the fact that this same investment of a million a-year, instead of regenerating our fields, returns to us for interest the threat, at least, of death to the thousands who are compelled to inhale the poisonous gases which escape, it will be allowed that the Chinese have something to say for their primitive, simple, effective, and yet very offensive method of getting rid of the nuisance.

丐高雲集

唱蓮花郎

STREET BEGGARS.

STREET BEGGARS.

BEGGARS form a numerous fraternity in China. In some parts of the country they constitute a powerful body, and boast of an independent government, under their own king. A distinction, however, must be drawn between those who are compelled to beg from sheer poverty, or misfortune, and those who have made choice of begging as a profession. The aged, the blind (at least those of them who do not gain a livelihood by fortune-telling), the widow with her fatherless children, the lame, and the infirm, may be seen at the corners of streets, imploring in piteous tones an alms of the passer-by. Sometimes, when a flood devastates a tract of country, sweeping away the dwellings of hundreds of the inhabitants, or when, by the failure of the crops of a district, food rises to famine price, then formidable gangs of men, women, and children appear, levying contributions on the more-favoured regions. Forlorn and miserable, these troops of half-famished vagrants take up their abode in any spot that promises an appearance of shelter, lodging in the watch-towers of the city walls, or even in the empty tombs of deserted burial grounds, and from their abodes of misery emerging with wild and threatening cries and entreaties for relief.

The beggars represented in our sketch are of the associated band of mendicants, whose character for profligacy is but too notorious. They are, by common report, slaves to every vice, especially to that of opium-smoking; and so necessary does this drug in some form become that, if times go hard with them, they are compelled to satisfy their cravings by smoking out the dregs of the exhausted opium-pipes, scraped together in the public divans. Their mode of extorting money is bold and systematic. A certain rate is arbitrarily imposed on the principal shops of a street: the rate being levied and paid, there is an exemption from further importunity, guaranteed by the exhibition of a red ticket, which is a sign to the fraternity that the " black mail" has been levied and paid. Where this red ticket has not been given, and the terms of compact have not been submitted to, the shop is open to their assault. The sum which they by clamour impudently extort is small in amount—a single coin, in value about the thirtieth part of a penny, is a sufficient exemption from further molestation, at least for the day. Their weapons of importunity are fearfully effective. Peace and quietness fly from the presence of these men, armed with instruments which emit the most annoying and disagreeable sounds. No customer can make himself understood to the shopman while these rattles, accompanied by some wild cries, are going; and the rate which is not given in love is submissively tendered under this noisy menace. This the very matter-of-fact-looking person in our sketch is in the act of doing. That peculiar attitude in pushing the coin with the two fingers, and that imperturbable and self-satisfied air, are thoroughly characteristic of the Chinaman.

The noises made by these rattles are of many kinds. Sometimes a few copper coins of the country are turned rapidly round in a metal or Chinaware basin; a simple construction, which the reader, if curious, may test by thus turning, with a dexterous movement of the wrist, a few farthings in a common bowl. Sometimes a piece of large bamboo is struck with a stout stick; sometimes, again, pieces of wood, like castanets, are made to produce a clacking sound; sometimes, pieces of brass are beaten together; all of them very simple creations of the mischievous faculty in man, and rivalling each other in power of sending forth the most grating and discordant sounds. Provided with these, they are truly masters of the situation, and levy their extortions, undisturbed by the frowns or more active interference of the civil magistrate. I must beg the reader to mark the braided queue (vulgò tail) of both the mendicant figures, bound over their caps. This is a common sign of active employment, hardihood, and energy. All with whose occupations the long, pendant tail would interfere, carefully coil it up, using it, in fact, as a fastening to keep the cap on the head. The men of the province of Fokien, who longest resisted the Tartar mode of tonsure, still adopt the custom of binding their queues round their heads, and covering all over with a blue turban.

If any among this class of beggars violates the laws of order, save in the recognized and tolerated manner just described, he is amenable to the rules of his own community; and a representation made to the chief would entail on the offender immediate punishment. Thus their license is restrained within certain bounds, and though they may justly

be regarded as a great public nuisance, they are not
generally, in other respects, disturbers of the public
peace, at least in towns and populous districts. In
more retired quarters they are, however, apt to become formidable, and substitute plunder on a large
scale for the smaller extortions permitted, as we
have seen, in the populous localities. They will
even attack the traveller, and rob him if they can.
I know from personal experience that a bold demeanor is the best means of warding off their
attacks. Woe to the unfortunate traveller whose
expressed fears tempt these rude vagrants to an
assault. His purse is sure to suffer to the full
extent of its contents.

There is yet another class of mendicants, who
resort to the same expedients which are used among
ourselves for exciting compassion. A piteous tale
of distress is written with chalk on the pavement,
or painted on a square board; and the sufferer,
frantic with grief, will beat the head violently
against the hard stone, to move the pity of the passenger. It is as difficult, too, to distinguish simu-
lated from real distress, as it is in England. I
once took the trouble of causing a man, who pro-
fessed that his wrist had been nearly hacked
through in an engagement with pirates, to be car-

ried in a sedan chair to the dispensary of a medical friend, who, after due inspection, pronounced it a case for amputation. Preparations were actually made for the operation. A priest belonging to an adjoining Buddhist monastery was engaged to receive and nurse him till convalescent; the surgeon began to remove the bandage; amid the shrieks of the supposed sufferer, warm water was applied to soften the coagulated blood; roll after roll of the bandage was removed, until at last the wrist appeared stripped, but perfectly sound and whole. So ingeniously was the imposture contrived, that it thus at first deceived even the practised eye of a foreign surgeon.

It may be added to this sketch of Asiatic mendicancy, that the greater portion of the beggars of China are so from choice: a fact which is evinced in the common proverb, "The finest rice has not charms equal to a roving liberty."

測字

—

THE SYMBOLISM OF WORDS.

—•—

FORTUNE-TELLING has many different branches, each of which demands a long apprenticeship for its acquisition. For instance, the determination of lucky and unlucky days, calculated by the aspect of particular stars and planets, is a definite study and pursuit. It would be a mistake to suppose it all mere guess-work, or all mere conscious imposture; it is regarded as a science, and the majority of those who practise it persuade themselves of its truth. In the Imperial Almanack of each year, which is, as it were, an accredited Moore's almanack, are recorded under every month what days are good for consummating marriages, for commencing journeys, for opening schools, for building houses, for dedicating temples, &c. But this authoritative publication does not interfere with the practice of the occult art by private individuals, who not only deal with some general principles of astrology, but who are also ready to give

information on any event over which futurity holds
her dark and impenetrable veil.   In the case of
betrothment, the horoscope of the two affianced
parties is previously examined; the year, the month,
the day, the hour,* of their birth is accurately
noted; and by two signs belonging to each of
these four periods of the year, the propriety of
completing the engagement is determined.   If
anything very fearful and forbidding should appear in the two horoscopes, the proposed agreement would not be carried out; it would not be
thought prudent to run counter to the plainly-
expressed opinion of the powers above.

Fortune-tellers of every kind find constant employment.   Their shops are seldom empty; for the
Chinese mind, ignorant or forgetful of the doctrine
of a supreme and ever-ruling Providence, is always
finding occasions to consult these astrologers and
mystery-mongers.

Our picture represents a kind of fortune-telling
which is much in vogue, the employment of which
reveals the literary character of the nation.   A
number of important and significant words are first
selected; each of these are then written upon a

---

* " Hour." This is a division of time consisting of two hours.
Every day is divided into twelve parts, called sze tsing.

THE SYMBOLISM OF WORDS.

separate slip of thin card-board, which is made-up
into a roll, like those very tiny scrolls of parch-
ment, inscribed with a verse of scripture, which
are used at the present day by the Jews in their
phylacteries. These slips of card-board, amounting
altogether to several hundreds, are shaken together
in a box; and the consulting party—moved, perhaps,
with solicitude to know the result of an intended
expedition, or a coming engagement in business,—
repairing to the fortune-teller who is always to be
found at some convenient corner of a street, puts
in his hand and draws from the box one of these
scrolls of paper. The mysteries of the art are
now displayed; the fortune-teller, writing the significant word on a white board which he keeps at
his side, begins to discover its root and derivation,
shows its component parts, explains where its em-
phasis lies, what its particular force is in composition, and then deduces from its meaning and structure some particulars, which he applies to the
special case of the consulter. No language, perhaps, possesses such facilities for diviners and their
art as the Chinese; and the words selected are
easily made to evolve, under the manipulation of a
skilful artist, some mystical meaning of oracular
indefiniteness. Some faint notion of this method

of divination may be gathered from remarking the change of meaning which, in our own and other languages, arises from the transposition of the letters forming a name or sentence. For instance, the name Horatio Nelson becomes, by a happy alliteration, Honor est a Nilo. Again, Vernon becomes Renown, and Waller, Laurel. Or in the remarkable instance of Pilate's question, Quid est veritas, which by transposition gives, Est vir qui adest.

Now let the reader fix his eye on our sketch. Here is the diviner engaged in his functions. He is seated within a frame, on the front board of which is written, in Chinese, the words "Seek after the good omen ; avoid the evil destiny ;" and just before him is the box with its scrips of ominous import, on which, also, are inscribed laudations of his own proficiency in the art—the art to fathom the meaning of words. The significant scroll has been drawn forth by the patient, and our diviner is in the act of separating it into its component parts, and explaining its meaning to the case in hand. See how our divining friend, evidently a master of his art, is glibly unfolding its hidden depths, while with his pencil he rapidly traces the lines which form the word.

The way in which he holds this pencil, seldom

properly attained by the foreigner, is etched with a life and accuracy which makes any description of mine unnecessary. That lantern in front will be lit at night, when the vermillion letters inscribed on the transparent paper will attract the attention of the passers-by, and invite them to try the fortune-teller's skill. The countenance of the countryman shows a quiet stupidity and good-humour, very characteristic of the northener, inhabiting the low alluvial plains of Chekeang. The never-failing lantern rests by his side, ready to light him home if belated. Even on the full moon, if he be a careful Chinaman, he will not have omitted to bring it with him. He has thrown down his three copper cash (about half a farthing of our money), which is the fee demanded for the consultation. If he has lost no more than this, he may consider himself a fortunate man. Not that he will be cheated out of his money, for the trade is honestly conducted, and there is a fixed fee for each consultation; but that, instead of relying upon his own energy, and acting upon high principles of rectitude, he has exposed himself to the blight of evil surmisings and to many a temptation, by making himself a slave to superstitious fear. The scene we have just described is as ancient as it is common. I have no doubt that every day for the last 2000 years, similar scenes have appeared in every part of China. And at present they are repeatedly seen by the side of a thronged thoroughfare, or in the open space between the outer and inner gate of a Chinese city, where crowds are constantly moving to and fro, in the pursuit of their business or amusement. The diviner and his stall are also sure to be seen at any great fair or religious festival, and generally wherever experience has taught men that the trade might be profitably plied. It is astonishing what a number of persons earn a livelihood by an occupation of which we should think every day's events would prove the fallacy. No one lifts up his voice against it. The Confucianist thinks it may be necessary for the rude, uneducated mind. Both the Buddhist and the Taonist encourage all feelings of dependence on the unseen world, as it is sure to bring a revenue to their monasteries. The state religion does indeed ridicule all such superstitions, but it is powerless to keep the people from practising them, nor do any of the influential men of the country see any sufficient reason to interfere. It is not (say they) a question of good government or good morals, it merely concerns a man's own mental convictions, and we may safely leave these to take their own course. A very favourite expression of theirs is, "If you believe, these things have reality; if you believe not, they have none." By which is meant, that every person must be guided by his own convictions; that the great matter is sincerity and earnestness, and that a false creed heartily embraced, where it does not oppose morality, will be of more use to restrain and govern than a barren orthodoxy.

CRYSTAL VASE.

A MOUNTAIN CARRIER.

送娘

THE MATCH-MAKERS.

THE MATCH-MAKERS.

IT is now pretty generally known to those at all familiar with the habits of China, that as a rule, no Chinese girl has any chance of continuing in single blessedness, and dying an old maid. Her destiny is usually determined very early in life. Except the nuns of Buddha and Taou, who are celibates of a very suspicious order, every woman in China above the age of twenty years is a wife, and if Heaven favour, a mother. The union of the two parties, who by the powers above have been destined for each other (for the proverb, marriages are made in heaven, obtains there as here), is not left to any fortuitous concurrence of events. The gentle season of wooing, so prolific of tender emotions, soft sayings, and delicate attentions, has not yet dawned on the youths and maidens of China. Match-making is a serious business, nay, a special function among the Chinese. All the preliminaries are effected, either by a common

N

friend of the families (*mei-jin*), or by a privileged
class of persons ("*sung-neang*"). Among the curiosities of Chinese real life, the functions of these
professional match-makers are not the least strange
and remarkable. These women are found only in
certain parts of China; none north of the Hang-
chow river; none, that I am aware of, without the
limits of the province of Chekeang.

A class of men called *do-be*—(by a singular coincidence the very same name which describes one of
the low castes of India)—were degraded from their
social position some four centuries back, as a
punishment for a revolt against the then-reigning
power. So tradition, rather than any authentic
history, has recorded. Against these men the road
to official promotion is barred. They are not permitted to enter the lists at the periodical literary
contests, nor are they allowed to make choice of
any trade or profession. The bearing of sedan-
chairs, the pedlar's weary round, the barber's
menial toil, and the stage, are the only means of
livelihood open to them. They intermarry with
one another; and their wives, debarred from social
intercourse with the daughters of the country,
have found that they can make themselves useful
in the singular occupation of effecting matrimonial

arrangements between the members of different families, moving in the same sphere of life. They may, perhaps, be more trusted in this employment because they can have no family interests of their own to serve. All that they look for by way of recompense is a certain sum of money for their good offices.

The engraving by our Chinese artist most accurately represents their appearance. They are dressed with the utmost plainness and neatness, and many of them are good-looking, which, however, is no recommendation to their virtue; their feet are " got up " in the height of the prevailing fashion. Though constantly exposed to all kinds of weather in the pursuit of their functions, they never wear bonnet, hat, or head-dress of any kind, save their own black hair with the glossy " butterflies' wings "* at the back of the head. Wet or fine they always carry an umbrella, which has a particularly long handle, and serves the double use of protection from rain and a walking-stick; a small bundle of blue and white check, containing a change of shoes, or some article of dress or ornament, completes the outfit. Each has, either by law, or by custom powerful as law, a district as-

* " Butterflies' wings," see sketch, The Collector of Hair.

signed to her; over this she travels at certain
periods, and endeavours to effect matrimonial al-
liances between the families whom she visits. Often
the agreement has been previously made by the
families themselves without her assistance; in
which case her services are only needed on the
few days previous and subsequent to the day of
marriage, when she is ready to support the bride
when she worships with her bridegroom-elect
before the ancestral shrine, or receives the con-
gratulations of her visitors, and to accompany her
when she, according to custom, subsequent to marriage, pays her visits of ceremony to the houses of
her friends. If any have been accustomed to think
of the Chinese women as so crippled by the process
of binding the foot as to be unable to walk, let him
learn to correct, or at least to modify his opinion
by the picture now before him. Here are women,
with feet in the extreme of fashion, who yet daily
go their rounds in the prosecution of their trade.
There is, doubtless, some inconvenience felt, especially by those who do not accustom themselves to
walking; but the accounts given of the evil conse-
sequences of crippled feet are much exaggerated;
and if that suggestion were true, that the fathers
and husbands introduced this fashion in order to

keep their wives and daughters from gadding about, all we can say is, that they have miserably failed in their attempt. Of the thousands of women who crowd the Buddhist temples on gala days, or who make pilgrimages to sacred shrines in the country, by far the greater part travel almost literally *on* their ten toes, eight of which are doubled up underneath the foot.

We are by no means, however, apologists, much less advocates for the fashion, any more than for the flattening of the heads, or the contracting of the waists, which yet prevail in some countries only partially civilized; and it will be well for China's daughters when this barbarous custom, which originated from the Imperial palace, and spread by the irresponsible law of fashion, shall in the same way cease to be followed. The popular feeling at present is so strong for its use, that these "*sung-neang*" would find it very difficult to obtain a husband for a large-footed damsel. However beautiful her features might be, yet this stigma of vulgarity would be an effectual barrier to her matrimonial prospects. It would be regarded as a sure sign of low extraction, possibly of an abandoned life; some Tartar or European influence would be suspected, or some connection with the despised nuns of the religious sects.

What a strange view does the match-maker present of Chinese life! How differently constituted must their society be from our own which can endure an institution like this! With what eyes would a young Englishman look upon one of these traders as she emerged from a neighbour's house? He would be miserable under the thought that preliminaries of marriage might have been just settled and his fate in life sealed. The youth in China, however, seldom has spirit enough to resist this tyrannical law of social life. He submits with as good grace as may be to the appointment, and performs his matrimonial engagement as a necessary filial duty. When, through shyness or other cause, he might have incurred the charge of deepest filial impiety—the absence of children—the match-maker comes to his aid, and helps him out of his difficulty.

No one need ask about the results of a system like this. It is the prolific parent of domestic bickering. Save in a few exceptional cases, there is no congeniality of sentiment, no reciprocity of sweet affection between husband and wife.

The institution, however, must and will continue unaltered while woman remains uneducated, and where the wife is not regarded as the fit companion and adviser of her husband. The only power which can expel the "*sung-neang*" from the cities and villages which she now occupies, is the higher estimate of the character and duties of woman. The Chinese in their novels are not without this idea; they wait to be taught that it may become, under Christian teaching, the rule of common life, instead of an exception of romance.

A COUNTRY WOMAN.

A MARRIAGE PROCESSION.

No. 26.

THE ROLL OF THE NAMES OF HONOUR.

THE ROLL OF THE NAMES OF HONOUR.

OF the four cardinal pleasures mentioned by the Chinese, one is "to see your name on the roll of honour."* A distinction which well repays all the study and anxiety of the previous ten, twenty, or thirty years bestowed to attain it.

Nothing is so much coveted by a man, either for himself or his children, as this, and the higher honours and emoluments to which it may lead.

The list of the successful candidates is at first placarded in front of the great examination hall, where the two thousand students of the district have lately sat, undergoing their trial. It is affixed also to the outer wall of the mandarin's office, where crowds soon gather to con over its contents, hoping to find the name of some relative or friend among those who have earned distinction in the contest.

* The other three are—
  In time of drought to see refreshing rain ;
  In a strange place to meet a bosom friend ;
  The candles lighted in the marriage hall.

An office like that represented in our picture meets with ready support. As soon as the list has been made public, and can again be printed off, our lively friend, putting on his cap of etiquette with the red tassel, armed with a gong, and gifted with a stentorian voice, proclaims through the smaller towns and retired country villages, that he has the true and genuine list of these names of merit for sale, and finds many, who, from interest or mere curiosity, are willing to become purchasers.

It is no mean honour to have obtained even the first grade in the ladder of promotion; and parents are highly gratified if their child be found among thirty or forty foremost names of the two thousand who once every three years contend for the degree of *siew tsai*.   This honour and this delight are, of course, intensified in proportion to the value of the degree obtained.

The first grade confers the privilege of wearing a certain dress at the formal visit of the examining commissioners, and of having a gold button to the cap; the second grade places the fortunate competitor in the way of obtaining office under Government. A higher step still, attainable only by a visit to the capital, makes him a marked man, even among millions; for the family which had a member of the degree of *tsing sze* would be known throughout a whole province; while he who advanced higher still, and came out the first name of all in the Imperial College of Han-lin would be known throughout the whole land, and all classes would delight to do him honour. These wandering heralds of his fame bear on the flag at their backs his name, which is thus blazoned abroad through all the districts of the eighteen provinces; nor is there a village, however far removed from the ordinary intercourse of life, which will not learn some particulars of his history. His own native place is especially proud to do him service, and is never tired of proclaiming the honour which his talents have conferred upon it; and when he moves abroad, the inns by the way-side, at which he halts, or the Buddhist monasteries, which lodge him for the night, never forget to boast of their distinguished guest.

It is easy to conceive how great must be the stimulus which this Chinese system gives to learning. There is no difficulty in inducing parents to send their boys to school. Even the poorest find money to do this, hoping that their son may show such an amount of talent as will put him in the position either of a schoolmaster or private tutor;

or that he may even rise above the first grade of academical distinction, and become, by successive steps, a magistrate, a judge, a secretary of state, or even a prime minister. The children, too, easily susceptible of praise, are urged on by many graphic stories of men, great in their country's history, who have raised themselves to positions of eminence by application and perseverance. These are now becoming familiar to the English reader. Of this kind is the story of the youth, who, too poor to buy a candle, managed, through a chink in his neighbour's partition wall, to study his task by night. Another, under similar pressure of poverty, is said to have confined in a glass-bottle a firefly, by the light of which he conned his midnight task. The account given of a third is, that he fastened his long queue to the beam above him, that when, overcome by fatigue, he nodded over his task, he might be roused to fresh exertion. The sequel to these tales, of course, is that the hard-working student emerges from his poverty, and becomes a hero in the annals of his country. And when these tales appear too childish for the advancing student, there are never wanting living examples of those who are reaping the golden fruits of their untiring industry, to excite his emulation.

The Chinese very early commenced with this competitive system, and they have practised it successfully for many centuries. The incoming of the Manchow power produced no change in this respect. The foreign conqueror acted most wisely in tying his yoke upon the necks of the people with the soft and silken cord of their own most valued institution.

Literary merit, notwithstanding the increasing number of cases of bribery, is still the real ground of promotion. Any great departure from this rule invariably brings down the wrath of the people upon the head of the offending magistrate; and most serious disaffection will certainly follow any general departure from old-established principle and practice. Many, indeed, trace the disturbances, which for the last ten years have been threatening the overthrow of the Manchow dynasty, to the fact, that wealth, rather than merit, is, in so many cases, becoming the step to official promotion.

ANCIENT CHINESE VASE.

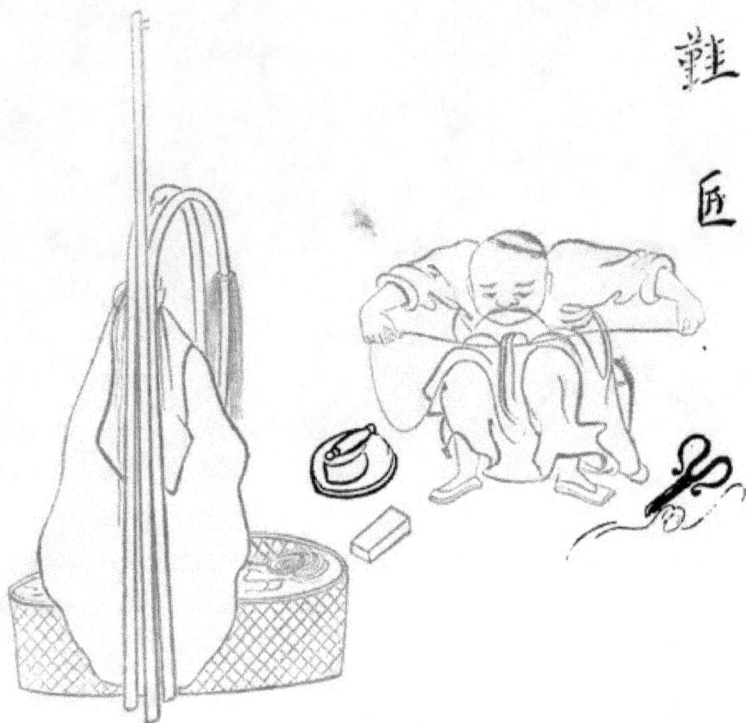

鞋
匠

THE COBBLER.

THE COBBLER; OR, A CHAPTER ON SHOES.

WE have before us, imported from the shores of a land whose sun rises eight hours before our own, a figure, which, at the first glance, we all recognize. No one need look at the heading of this sketch, or read a line of our description—he knows at once that he is looking at a cobbler.

Who could mistake that peculiar attitude? The waxed thread has just been drawn through by both hands, and the double-stitch is being tightened to its extreme tension. The shoe is held between the knees in most approved cobbler fashion; and, with the exception of the peculiar Chinese features and Tartar tonsure, the figure might serve for any member of the craft in Europe.

In China, the advantage of division of labour is well understood. Shoe-making, shoe-mending, and shoe-selling are distinct branches.

No shop is more neat and inviting than that of a boot and shoe manufactory. There is none of that unpleasant odour of the leather, which makes a similar shop amongst us so disagreeable; for, except in the hob-nailed shoe used in wet weather, there is but little leather employed in the construction of a Chinese shoe.

All its component parts are—for the top and sides, calico, silk, satin, or velvet; and for the soles, several layers of thick felt.

Shoes in China exhibit great varieties, in their material, shape, and workmanship,

The lowest kind is the straw sandal worn by coolies, which merely protects the sole of the foot from injury, and is fastened by a band of straw over the instep.

Next to this is a light shoe, much worn by merchant pedestrians in the country, made of rushes; some, for greater durability, are interwoven with coarse cotton, and bound with narrow ribbon. Then comes the common shoe, formed of different kinds of material, according to the means or fancy of the wearer. It is usually made of dark calico, and the toe adorned with pieces of cotton velvet.

The wealthier classes prefer satin, the sides and

toes being embroidered elaborately in silk. The
sole is the same thickness throughout, formed of
three, four, five, six, or even seven layers of felt,

which is sometimes protected by a thin outer sole
of leather. This thick sole is whitened with pipe-
clay, and so cleaned.

The soldier's shoe is very peculiar in shape,
and is easily recognized by its long pointed toe.

If tipped with iron, we could imagine this to be
a more formidable weapon than the clumsy spear
and matchlock of native warfare.

The common shoe of the children is made of
brown or purple calico, bound with red, and worked

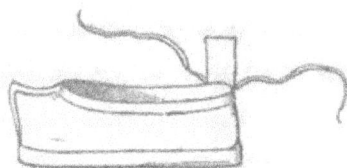

up the toe with coloured silk; the sole is formed
of layers of coarse cloth stitched together. It is
usually made by the female members of a household.

o

The children of the wealthier class generally wear shoes of scarlet satin, often highly embroidered, and pointed at the toe with ears and eyes, to resemble a tiger's head.

Another kind is the children's summer shoe, made of fine open rush-work, with a gay coloured lining, and the toe stitched with little pieces of velvet and gold thread, to look like a butterfly.

I must not altogether omit a description of the ladies' shoes, though these are all made and mended by themselves, and, therefore, do not properly belong to the province of our cobbler. The best thing I can do is to add a drawing of a shoe fitted to receive the "golden lily," for such is the polite synonym for the foot of the Chinese woman.

UNBOUND FOOT.

THE FASHION.

I dare not say to what extremes fashion may go

in other parts of China.   By actual measurement
I find the length of the women's shoe, about
Ningpo, to be three-and-a-half inches from the
heel to toe.

All I have now described, and I have by no
means exhausted the catalogue, are what are called
"dry" shoes; they are intended only for dry weather, and have little or no leather about them.
They are well adapted for the paved roads which
universally prevail on the Ningpo plain.

The rain-shoe, intended for wet weather, does not
differ much in shape from those in ordinary use.
It is, however, made altogether of leather, and is
raised at least half-an-inch from the ground by iron
pegs, which look very like the large stud-nails on
the doors of churches.   The poorer classes, in wet
weather, often use a shoe with an inch-thick sole of
wood, well deserving the name of our exploded
clog.   As only the sole is of wood, and the upper
part of some soft material, this is greatly preferable
to the wooden shoes of the Dutch sailors.

The shoes described above are all soft and easy
to the feet.   The foreigner who begins to wear
them, finds that he can scarcely again bear the
hard leather of his own boot.   Corns and bunions

those plagues of an over-civilization, are almost unknown. The women alone seem to suffer much from them.

As it is intimately connected with this subject of shoes, I may describe an ingenious use to which the Chinese put old rags. One very common employment of women and children is, the pasting of bits of old rag on a board or shutter, till they are of the thickness of strong pasteboard, which are dried in the sun, then stripped off the board, and cut up into soles for the commoner kinds of shoes ; one great reason why girls cannot be retained at the day-schools of the missionaries, is their employment at this work. They begin very early to be useful ; for it does not require much strength of body or of mind to paste one rag of calico on the top of another.

The cobbler who heads this paper goes his rounds from street to street, and announces his presence with the rattle peculiar to his calling. He carries in his basket, on his back, all the implements necessary to his trade ; a large piece of leather, more used in mending than in making shoes, a pair of uncouth scissors, a large knife, a stone on which to sharpen it, his wax, thread, needles, brad-awls, and the other implements necessary to his functions. If your shoes are in need of repair, you do not send them to the shoe-maker's shop, but watch for the sound of the cobbler's rattle, and if you call him in, he will sit at work in your court-yard, and do what you want, both cheaply and expeditiously.

MEN'S SHOES.

PAGODA ISLAND.

賣混沌

THE COOK-SHOP.

NO less than four of the pen-and-ink etchings of
my Chinese friend relate to the culinary art.
Photography itself could hardly exceed in accuracy
these drawings. They are correct representations
of some of the commonest phases of street-life in
China; not pictures got up for the occasion, but
scenes from every-day life. A stall, like that en-
graved on the opposite page, is carried on the back
of the owner, and set down at some convenient
corner of a street, where it remains till purchasers
have exhausted its contents. Such are frequently
found at a late hour of night, or even past the
fourth watch, in the hope of catching some stray
customer returning from business in the country,
or some *roué* from the haunts of dissipation, who,
enlivened by the fumes of opium, feels the keen
edge of returning appetite. I cannot attempt to
describe all the contents of the boiler in this pic-

ture, all that the different teapots and the eight small drawers contain. They are known only to the initiated, and many of them have no nomenclature among ourselves. If I may give the result of occasional investigation, I should say that the chief article of food which here tempts the palate, consists of very small rice-flour dumplings, stuffed with a sweet confectionery, and stewed in sweet-sauce. The stooping figure, who appears to be smoking a pipe, is, in reality, blowing up his wood or charcoal fire with his cheap and simple bellows. This instrument is constructed of a tube of bamboo with a small hole perforated at the joint. The stream of air exhaled from the lungs is thus concentrated upon one point without any waste of breath or needless puffing. For the furnaces of the ironmonger a much more effective bellows is used, which will be described in our account of the Brazier.

By the two paper lanterns attached to the portable cook-shop, we are reminded that the owner is preparing to open his *restaurant* for evening customers. His appearance and dress tell the tale of his own slender means. Seldom can he afford to taste the sweet and rich compounds which his customers devour. A bowl of boiled rice, with a relish

賣石花

THE COOK-SHOP.—No. 2.

To face p. 201.

of salted vegetable, green or brown sea-weed, is his staple for breakfast, dinner, and supper. He does not, however, murmur at his lot; but rather, as he thrusts the contents of his bowl into his capacious mouth with two sticks, it may be extemporized for the occasion, he doubtless felicitates himself that he lives within the borders of a rice-producing district, and finds satisfaction in pitying the hard fate of the poor foreigner, obliged to live all his days upon hard bread or biscuit, varied occasionally with a slice of tough and half-roasted mutton or beef.

Whatever may be said by others against Chinese living, I will venture to state my conviction that there are few countries which produce such a variety of cheap and good food as China; fewer still which will bear comparison with her people in the art of cooking. Although no mutton or beef is used at the tables of the wealthy, yet the variety of *entrées* is hardly exceeded by any nobleman's table in England; nor have English and American merchants thought it beneath them to invite a party to dinner entirely "*à la Chinois,*" save only in the use of plates instead of the smooth, polished table, and the substitution of spoon and forks for chopsticks. Knives are never required at a Chinese feast, nor are they ever seen in polite

society, but are confined to the purlieus of the
kitchen. As to cooking, while it is generally a
strong point with the people, the perfection of the
art is nowhere more observable than in the monasteries of the Buddhists. They have but the sim-
plest elements of food to deal with. No meat, no
fish, no poultry, are allowed at their tables. No
eggs, no lard, no butter, no milk, must be introduced in their confectionery. Vegetables alone are
permitted; and yet by means of these a dinner of
surprising variety is served up to table; and if the
guest judged only by appearances, he would suppose that the worthy abbot had forgotten the rigid
rules of his monastic establishment, and was about
to break his vow by partaking of most heretical
viands.

Foreigners who have travelled much in the interior of China, and have so far had faith in Chinese
food as to leave their own baskets of provisions
behind them, will bear their testimony to the great
convenience of stalls like those represented in the
accompanying engravings. You can seldom find
a village which is too poor to supply something
hot in the way of refreshment. No one as he travels, even in rural districts, need fear starvation. It
may be only the simple bean-soup or bean-cakes

賣豆漿

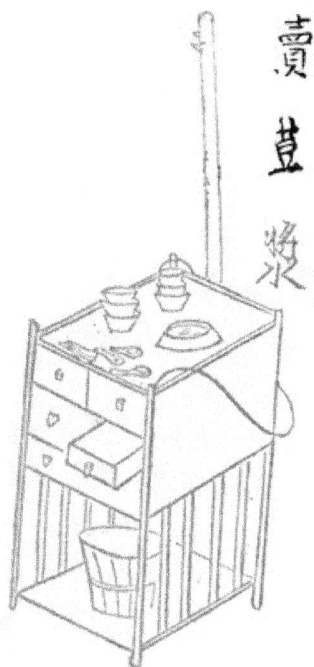

THE COOK-SHOP.—No. 3.

To face p. 202.

賣湯圓

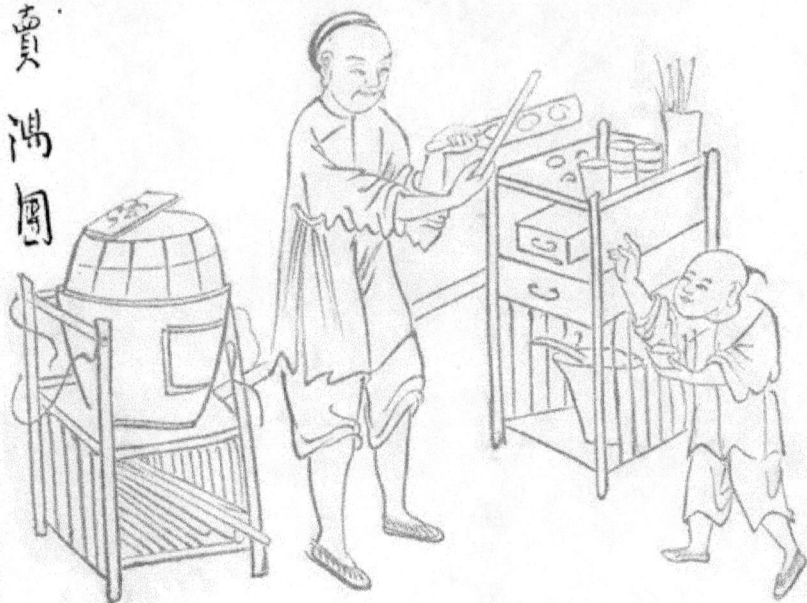

THE COOK-SHOP.—No. 4.

To face p. 203.

which are offered, or the three-cornered *no-me* rice-puddings, boiled in a wrapper of the plantain-leaf, and eaten with coarse sugar; or, again, something in the way of sausages—pork and onion chopped fine, with bread-crumbs and white of eggs to give consistency, made up into balls of the size of a large walnut—these, with bowls of steaming hot rice, will satisfy the cravings of appetite. As you continue your journey, here a stall tempts you with steamed buns of wheat-flour, filled with small dice of fat pork and lumps of sugar; or, if you need lighter food still, cakes and biscuits in great variety, and sweetmeats of every form, put forward their claims.

Earthworms and snails, rats, kittens, and puppies, though frequent in the pages of travellers in China, are fortunately rare in Chinese markets and on Chinese cook-stalls. No one need fear freely to indulge in the dishes set before him. Palatable they may not always be—for that "tastes differ" has passed into a proverb—still he may rest assured that the sensual Chinaman will not greatly offend against the laws of *gourmanderie*.

A CAMEL-DRIVER.

賣
雞
鴨
鵝
鴨

THE MARKET-MAN.

THE MARKET-MAN.

THE Biographer of Mr. Samuel **Budgett**, **in** his work called "The Successful **Merchant**," states that, when **Mr. B.** was a boy at school, he found that, "by buying a pennyworth of marbles, and **selling** to his schoolfellows in two half-penny-worths, **he could** honestly **gain two** marbles." Lozenges, also, by **the same law, were found** to yield similar results; **and the** boy, being possessed **with a strong** mercantile spirit, was, as his brother **says,** perpetually trading. The Buddhists would easily explain this phenomenon of life: they would assert that Mr. **B.** had been a pedler in a former state of existence, and that "the cask had retained its **odour**" **even to** another birth into being, and thus the mercantile spirit, born with him **and** setting in with a strong flood from his earliest childhood, carried him forward in a successful line **of** business till **he** attained **a** high position of **wealth** and influence.

The Chinese, by the same convenient law of transmigration, show that in some former " *culpa*" or age, they were all a nation of small merchants. Nothing has greater charms for them than a bargain. In all smaller transactions there is no hope of securing a purchase on fair terms without much higgling about the price to be paid. The law of wholesale and retail dealing is nowhere better understood; careful scraping together of small coin is nowhere more generally practised, though perhaps even they might learn a lesson of our "Successful Merchant," who, as we read, began his mercantile career "by begging and obtaining leave from his mother to scrape together the treacle which ran over to waste and sell it for himself."

Almost every Chinaman is, by a kind of natural instinct, good both at cooking and at bargaining. It is in the latter capacity more especially that we have now to speak of him, though we cannot help being reminded of the former also by the contents of the baskets before us.

The scene represented in our etching is common to every Chinese street on a market-day. The figure with the steel-yard is purveyor in some gentleman's family—possibly a cook in some foreigner's house. He is evidently made up for work; his cap is tightly bound to his head with his plaited queue, which serves this and many other useful purposes; his purse, made of stout cotton cloth, finished off at the corner with tassels, is slung over his shoulder. It contains the cumbrous coinage of the country—strings of a thousand copper coins, divided into hundreds for the convenience of trade. He is girt for his work: a blue or black sash gathers his long robe round his loins, so that the free motion of his limbs is not impeded. The other figure is that of the market-man, who has brought his poultry into the city for sale. That they are both good at a bargain, and will not do discredit to their national character, no one can doubt who marks the expression of their countenances, which tells us that a dispute is taking place as to the weight of the poultry, or as to the price to be paid for them. The steel-yard, consisting of a mahogany rod marked at different distances by small brass studs, is in the act of being used to weigh the struggling poultry. This steel-yard is a source of perpetual strife between buyer and seller. There is no officer appointed by Government, like our inspector, to regulate weights and measures. Every householder has his own steel-yard differently graduated; so that the seller of the goods has to look closely after his own interest. Here is a fine field for one imbued with the mercantile spirit! He will find both his talent and his temper constantly exercised. A Billingsgate fishwife has passed into a proverb with us; but in China every street on a market-day is a Billingsgate, and unseemly rancour constantly disturbs the quiet of the householder. The foreigner has no chance in this strife with the Chinaman; he does not attempt to compete with him in this respect, but secures, if possible, the services of one who will only take the accustomed percentage off the bargain transactions of the daily market. Happy may he consider himself who has a servant so far honest that he will keep within the reasonable bounds of ten per cent. profit on all purchases, and who professes, besides this amiable quality, that he will not suffer any one but himself to impose upon his master!

Many very amusing scenes do the markets of China offer to the observation of the foreigner. Our friend in the picture, if he had not succeeded in selling his poultry in the forenoon, would sit before them, making up balls of moistened pollard, and then proceed to thrust these down their throats. There is no concealment about this; it is done in

the face of the whole market, and is considered a
legitimate mode of increasing both their bulk and
weight. By a deception, even worse than this,
flabby fish are made to appear plump and good—
a reed is inserted, and they are then blown out,
so as to present a marketable appearance. When
a purchaser of the poultry arrives, the struggling
chicken, duck, or goose is seized by the feet, and
being firmly bound by a wisp of twisted straw, is
hung on to the steel-yard to be weighed. If the
price is agreed upon, the purchaser transfers the
suspended fowl from the hook of the steel-yard to
repose in the bottom of his own basket. Are you
a customer seeking for fish, you will find abundance;
chiefly large carp, swimming about in flat tubs.
These are all ringed ready for sale. If you name
the size you want, the fishmonger instantly pounces
upon one, suspends it by the string which is passed
through the nose, and deposits it by the side of the
chicken in the basket.

The market supplies you with a great variety of
good provision. Here are snake-like eels wriggling
and intertwining in large pans; there pails of
oysters without their shells, just brought, on the
backs of strong coolies, a distance of twenty miles.
Here, again, are crabs of every size, from the little

P

brown variety, which, for two months in the year, are eaten raw and *alive*, being merely dipped into a saucer of vinegar on their way to your mouth; or, if you prefer them, there is the large kind which have been preserved in brine, and which, like the beef-hams of America, to cook is to spoil. On that side you will find *béche de mer*, or its counterfeit, the skin of the pig stewed in oil, which tempt the palate of the epicure. More tempting still, and a more expensive luxury, are the bright green frogs which peep at you from the rush-bottomed baskets, and greet you with a croak; and the brown turtle or land-tortoise, whose hawk-like mouths are secured, lest they should grip the finger of the purchaser. There, again, are cockles, periwinkles, muscles, and other nameless shell-fish piled in baskets. All alive, or packed in ice, or preserved in salt, are fish, large and small, good and bad, adapted to the means of all customers. The cuttle-fish swims in its own inky liquid, tempting the man of moderate means, who cannot afford the richer delicacies. Of poorer food still, there are the different kinds of sea-weed, brown and green; or refuse shrimps dried and salted, forming a cheap relish for the cottager's rice. All vegetable produce is there—sweet potatoes, yams, taros, turnips, carrots, beans, peas, and cabbages, melons and cucumbers, according to the season.

On the butchers' stalls hangs flabby pork, which skill in cooking makes fit for the table of the epicure. If you must have mutton and beef, and if no foreign community have called this into requisition, that stall by the side of the street will supply you with cow-beef, stewed tender, at a cheap rate. If you must have mutton or lamb, you may have to put up with the flesh of the goat or kid, until a sufficient number of European residents have called for a supply.

A sufficiency of good food will be found in most markets to satisfy your utmost need. Only send out a trusty and clever servant in the early morning, with a few strings of copper coins in his money-bag, and he will bring you home a supply, which, with that other indispensable member of a household—a good cook—will make such a dinner as would content even the most fastidious of all deities.

A TEA PORTER.

銅

匠

THE BRAZIER.

—

THE BRAZIER.

———•———

INGENUITY is a gift largely bestowed upon the Chinaman; it is, indeed, one of his most marked characteristics—but it is ingenuity of that peculiar kind which works with very slender materials.

"*Multum in parvo*" would form an appropriate motto on the boxes of all the community of hawkers; it would be peculiarly appropriate over our engravings of the cook-shop, nor is it much less so in our present etching.

Our travelling tinker, or brazier, belongs to no roving gipsy tribe, so as to afford us materials of interest in habits of life, feelings, language, religion, &c. He is one of the people, and differs in nothing from their ordinary character. Yet our sketch may prove one of considerable interest, if we can but understand the neat little contrivances and appliances for the execution of the tinker's work. This shall be my attempt in this paper, though I rather fear falling into the matter-of-fact style of the encyclopædist.

The two oblong boxes contain everything necessary for the working-brazier's trade : they form, indeed, a complete laboratory. With these by his side, the tinker seeks for no extraneous aid, save, it may be, a few sticks of charcoal, which every household readily supplies. These boxes are carried at the intersection of the tough bamboo splines by the stout hooked pole, which appears at the back. As the tinker jogs along, seeking for employment, those pieces of brass, which dangle on a string, strike against each other and save him the exercise of his voice; they serve him the purpose of a street-cry. Every trade has its own particular rattle or call, and this of the tinker is as effectual, that is, as noisy, as any. The auger described in the sketch of the Needle-maker, which works backwards and forwards by means of a winding cord or thong, something like the spinning-mill of children, is seen hanging on the frame of the box. This instrument drills its holes with great speed and accuracy, and is used by most of the trades. The mender of broken pottery employs it with much success in preparing holes for the metal rivets with which he fastens the cracked or broken cup, tumbler, flower-glass, or lamp-globe, which native or foreigner may consign to his care. The carpenter could not carry on his work without its aid : it serves him instead of a dozen gimblets. The brazier finds it indispensable in all his mendings of broken pots and pans. The top of one of the boxes is fitted with a strong file working in a slide ; files of a smaller size will be found among the other tools in the drawers. The box before which the tinker sits is called a "wind-box ;" it is his bellows, and as he draws the handle backwards and forwards with even motion, a continuous current of air rushes down the bamboo tube, and blows up the charcoal fire contained in the iron pan. There is only room for one drawer in this bellows-box, which, in the engraving, is represented open. The other is fitted up according to the common custom of the country, or the taste and fancy of the individual workman, and divided into several compartments, which contain his tools, hammers, pincers, nails, odd pieces of brass, lead, resin, soldering-irons, &c., &c.

The utensils, which are represented as broken, and lying ready for the exercise of the tinker's skill, deserve a few lines of description. One of these may, perhaps, be guessed from its shape. It is a kind of hookah for smoking tobacco through water. A small tube, movable at pleasure, descends into the water contained in the lower part of the bowl. A pinch of tobacco, reduced to a powder almost like snuff, is inserted by the finger and thumb in the top of the tube; a lighted paper-match being applied, in about half-a-dozen strong whiffs, the pipe is exhausted; the tube is removed, the ashes are blown out upon the boarded floor, and the pipe is again ready for use.

The other broken vessel is quite a curiosity in its way. It serves instead of a stove, and is used as a warming-pan for the feet in the cold season. Stoves, or open fire-places, for the purpose of warming apartments, are, so far as I have yet seen or heard, unknown, save in the north of China. The substitute for them is increase of clothing, and, among the women chiefly, one of these pans. They are very simple in construction and very effective. The size and form are seen in the drawing; the perforated lid is movable and fits on like the top of a saucepan. The fuel is peculiar; whoever the inventor is, he well deserves a patent. Fine charcoal dust is mixed with rice-water, or thin paste, or any gelatinous substance; when made sufficiently damp to bind together it is pressed into a small iron mould, and, turned out, is left to dry and harden in the sun. Each of them will weigh about two ounces. When the pan is used it is filled three-parts full with wood-ashes. Two or three of the charcoal balls are then laid in a clear fire, and when heated red-hot are put carefully into the bed of ashes, and lightly covered over with them. The lid is then put on, and the fire-balls will keep burning at a red heat *for twelve or fifteen hours*, without being touched. The quantity of charcoal consumed, extended as it is over so many hours, can do no injury to the most delicate constitution.

During all the past winter I have had one of these in constant use; experience proves it an invaluable aid to those who suffer from cold feet; it will serve either for the room, or it may be used in the carriage, or the deck of a steam-boat, or the pew of a cold church, and may conclude its services at night by lying for ten minutes under the bed-clothes, doing its work as a warming-pan, without trouble, expense, or danger. With Chinese nurses it is a great favourite; it serves to dry any damp towel or cloth, and even serves to iron out small articles of clothing. **It is carried** by a handle, which appears in our picture to be broken; upon this the tinker's art is next to be employed.

Nowhere is there so extensively ramified a system of pedler's work as in China. Not only **the** pedler **proper, who goes** about vending his tapes, buttons, ribbons, scissors, needles, hair-pins, **and a** thousand **and one other nicnacs,** chiefly **for the** ladies; **not** only the market-man, who goes his round with fruit, vegetables, or flowers; the confectioner, who carries about trays of cakes and biscuits, and who tempts your palate with iced sea-weed jelly in the heat of summer; not only the cook, who gratifies your taste with delicious stews, and shows you white balls of flour stuffed with sweetmeat dancing merrily in a luscious sauce; not only the fisherman, who appears with every variety of marine product, from the vile sea-weed to the magnificent *tsze-yu* fish; but in a word, every **trade** has its travelling representative. Is any crockery broken in your house, does any water-jar without require mending, **is a** patch needed in your cloth or leather shoe, is a tooth of **your** head aching, or does tea-pot or kettle need soldering? Only set your servant to watch, the particular "cry" which belongs to each trade will soon be heard, the artizan steps into your court-yard, and is soon busy at his work, and, provided always the sum to be paid has been previously settled, will soon complete it to your satisfaction.

CHINESE TOMB.

WOODFALL AND KINDER, PRINTERS, ANGEL COURT, SKINNER STREET, LONDON.

A FUNERAL PROCESSION.

ALBEMARLE STREET, LONDON.
January, 1860.

MR. MURRAY'S
GENERAL LIST OF WORKS.

ABBOTT'S (Rev. J.) Philip Musgrave; or, Memoirs of a Church of England Missionary in the North American Colonies. Post 8vo. 2s. 6d.

ABERCROMBIE'S (John, M.D.) Enquiries concerning the Intellectual Powers and the Investigation of Truth. *Fifteenth Edition*. Fcap. 8vo. 6s. 6d.

———————— Philosophy of the Moral Feelings. *Twelfth Edition*. Fcap. 8vo. 4s.

———————— Pathological and Practical Researches on the Diseases of the Stomach, &c. *Third Edition*. Fcap. 8vo. 6s.

ACLAND'S (Rev. Charles) Popular Account of the Manners and Customs of India. Post 8vo. 2s. 6d.

ADDISON'S WORKS. A New Edition, with a New Life and Notes. By Rev. Whitwell Elwin. 4 Vols. 8vo. *In preparation*.

ADOLPHUS'S (J. L.) Letters from Spain, in 1856 and 1857. Post 8vo. 10s. 6d.

ÆSCHYLUS. (The Agamemnon and Choephoroe.) Edited, with Notes. By Rev. W. Peile, D.D. *Second Edition*. 2 Vols. 8vo. 9s. each.

ÆSOP'S FABLES. A New Translation. With Historical Preface. By Rev. Thomas James, M.A. With 100 Woodcuts, by John Tenniel and J. Wolf. 26th *Thousand*. Post 8vo. 2s. 6d.

AGRICULTURAL (The) Journal. Of the Royal Agricultural Society of England. 8vo. 10s. *Published half-yearly*.

AMBER-WITCH (The). The most interesting Trial for Witchcraft ever known. Translated from the German by Lady Duff Gordon. Post 8vo. 2s. 6d.

ARABIAN NIGHTS ENTERTAINMENT. Translated from the Arabic, with Explanatory Notes. By E. W. Lane. A New Edition. Edited by E. Stanley Poole. With 600 Woodcuts. 3 Vols. 8vo. 42s.

ARTHUR'S (Little) History of England. By Lady Callcott. *Nineteenth Edition*. With 20 Woodcuts. Fcap. 8vo. 2s. 6d.

AUNT IDA'S Walks and Talks; a Story Book for Children. By a Lady. Woodcuts. 16mo. 5s.

AUSTIN'S (Sarah) Fragments from German Prose Writers. With Biographical Notes. Post 8vo. 10s.

———————— Translation of Ranke's History of the Popes of Rome. *Third Edition*. 2 Vols. 8vo. 24s.

B

ADMIRALTY PUBLICATIONS; Issued by direction of the Lords
Commissioners of the Admiralty:—

1. A MANUAL OF SCIENTIFIC ENQUIRY, for the Use of Travellers
in General. By Various Hands. Edited by Sir JOHN F. HERSCHEL,
Bart. *Third Edition*, revised by Rev. ROBERT MAIN. Woodcuts.
Post 8vo. 9s.

2. AIRY'S ASTRONOMICAL OBSERVATIONS MADE AT GREENWICH.
1836 to 1847. Royal 4to. 50s. each.

——— ASTRONOMICAL RESULTS. 1848 to 1857. 4to. 8s. each.

3. ——— APPENDICES TO THE ASTRONOMICAL OBSERVA-
TIONS.

1836.—I. **Bessel's Refraction** Tables.
II. **Tables for** converting Errors of R.A. and **N.P.D.** }8s.
into Errors of Longitude and Ecliptic P.D. }
1837.—I. Logarithms **of Sines** and Cosines to every Ten }
Seconds **of Time.** }8s.
II. Table for converting Sidereal into Mean Solar Time. }
1842.—Catalogue of 1439 Stars. 8s.
1845.—Longitude of Valentia. 8s.
1847.—Twelve Years' Catalogue of Stars. 14s.
1851.—Maskelyne's Ledger of Stars. 6s.
1852.—I. Description of the Transit Circle. 5s.
II. Regulations of the Royal Observatory. 2s.
1853.—Bessel's Refraction Tables. 3s.
1854.—I. Description of the Zenith Tube. 3s.
II. Six Years' Catalogue of Stars. 10s.
1856.—Description of the Galvanic Apparatus at Greenwich Observatory. 8s.

4. ——— MAGNETICAL AND METEOROLOGICAL OBSERVA-
TIONS. 1840 to 1847. Royal 4to. 50s. each.

——— MAGNETICAL AND METEOROLOGICAL RESULTS.
1848 to 1857. 4to. 8s. each.

5. ——— ASTRONOMICAL, MAGNETICAL, AND METEOROLO-
GICAL OBSERVATIONS, 1848 to 1857. Royal 4to. 50s. each.

6. ——— REDUCTION OF THE OBSERVATIONS OF PLANETS,
1750 to 1830. Royal 4to. 50s.

7. ——————————————— LUNAR OBSERVATIONS. 1750
to 1830. 2 Vols. Royal 4to. 50s. each.

8. BERNOULLI'S SEXCENTENARY TABLE. *London*, 1779. 4to.

9. BESSEL'S AUXILIARY TABLES FOR HIS METHOD OF CLEAR-
ING LUNAR DISTANCES. 8vo.

10. ——— FUNDAMENTA ASTRONOMIÆ: *Regiomontii*, 1818. Folio. 60s.

11. BIRD'S METHOD OF CONSTRUCTING MURAL QUADRANTS.
London, 1768. 4to. 2s. 6d.

12. ——— METHOD OF DIVIDING ASTRONOMICAL INSTRU-
MENTS. *London*, 1767. 4to. 2s. 6d.

13. COOK, KING, AND BAYLY'S ASTRONOMICAL OBSERVATIONS.
London, 1782. 4to. 21s.

14. EIFFE'S ACCOUNT OF IMPROVEMENTS IN CHRONOMETERS.
4to. 2s.

15. ENCKE'S BERLINER JAHRBUCH, for 1830. *Berlin*, 1828. 8vo. 9s.

16. GROOMBRIDGE'S CATALOGUE OF CIRCUMPOLAR STARS.
4to. 10s.

17. HANSEN'S TABLES DE LA LUNE. 4to. 20s.

17. HARRISON'S PRINCIPLES OF HIS TIME-KEEPER. PLATES.
1767. 4to. 5s.

18. HUTTON'S TABLES OF THE PRODUCTS AND POWERS OF
NUMBERS. 1781. Folio. 7s. 6d.

19. LAX'S TABLES FOR FINDING THE LATITUDE AND LONGI-
TUDE. 1821. 8vo. 10s.

ADMIRALTY PUBLICATIONS—*continued.*

20. LUNAR OBSERVATIONS at GREENWICH. 1783 to 1819. Compared with the Tables, 1821. 4to. 7s. 6d.

22. MASKELYNE'S ACCOUNT OF THE GOING OF HARRISON' WATCH. 1767. 4to. 2s. 6d.

21. MAYER'S DISTANCES of the MOON'S CENTRE from the PLANETS. 1822, 3s.; 1823, 4s. 6d. 1824 to 1835, 8vo. 4s. each.

23. ———— THEORIA LUNÆ JUXTA SYSTEMA NEWTONIANUM 4to. 2s. 6d.

24. ———— TABULÆ MOTUUM SOLIS ET LUNÆ. 1770. 4to. 5s.

25. ———— ASTRONOMICAL OBSERVATIONS MADE AT GOTTINGEN, from 1756 to 1761. 1826. Folio. 7s. 6d.

26. NAUTICAL ALMANACS, from 1767 to 1861. 8vo. 2s. 6d. each.

27. ———— SELECTIONS FROM THE ADDITIONS up to 1812. 8vo. 5s. 1834-54. 8vo. 5s.

28. ———— SUPPLEMENTS, 1828 to 1833, 1837 and 1838. 8vo. 2s. each.

29. ———— TABLE requisite to be used with the N.A. 1781. 8vo. 5s.

30. POND'S ASTRONOMICAL OBSERVATIONS. 1811 to 1835. 4to. 21s. each.

31. RAMSDEN'S ENGINE for DIVIDING MATHEMATICAL INSTRUMENTS. 4to. 5s.

32. ———— ENGINE for DIVIDING STRAIGHT LINES. 4to. 5s.

33. SABINE'S PENDULUM EXPERIMENTS to DETERMINE THE FIGURE OF THE EARTH. 1825. 4to. 40s.

34. SHEPHERD'S TABLES for CORRECTING LUNAR DISTANCES. 1772. Royal 4to. 21s.

35. ———— TABLES, GENERAL, of the MOON'S DISTANCE from the SUN, and 10 STARS. 1787. Folio. 5s. 6d.

36. TAYLOR'S SEXAGESIMAL TABLE. 1780. 4to. 15s.

37. ———— TABLES OF LOGARITHMS. 4to. 3l.

38. TIARK'S ASTRONOMICAL OBSERVATIONS for the LONGITUDE of MADEIRA. 1822. 4to. 5s.

39. ———— CHRONOMETRICAL OBSERVATIONS for DIFFERENCES of LONGITUDE between DOVER, PORTSMOUTH, and FALMOUTH. 1823. 4to. 5s.

40. VENUS and JUPITER: OBSERVATIONS of, compared with the TABLES. London, 1822. 4to. 2s.

41. WALES' AND BAYLY'S ASTRONOMICAL OBSERVATIONS. 1777. 4to. 21s.

42. WALES' REDUCTION OF ASTRONOMICAL OBSERVATIONS MADE IN THE SOUTHERN HEMISPHERE. 1764—1771. 1788. 4to. 10s. 6d.

BABBAGE'S (CHARLES) Economy of Machinery and Manufactures. *Fourth Edition.* Fcap. 8vo. 6s.

———— Ninth Bridgewater Treatise. 8vo. 9s. 6d.

———— Reflections on the Decline of Science in England, and on some of its Causes. 4to. 7s. 6d.

———— Views of the Industry, the Science, and the Government of England, 1851. *Second Edition.* 8vo. 7s. 6d.

BAIKIE'S (W. B.) Narrative of an Exploring Voyage up the Rivers Quorra and Tshadda in 1854. Map. 8vo. **16s.**

BANKES' (GEORGE) STORY OF CORFE CASTLE, with documents relating to the Time of the Civil Wars, &c. Woodcuts. Post 8vo. 10s. 6d.

BASSOMPIERRE'S Memoirs of his Embassy to the Court of England in 1626. Translated with Notes. 8vo. 9s. 6d.

BARROW'S (SIR JOHN) Autobiographical Memoir, including Reflections, Observations, and Reminiscences at Home and Abroad. From Early Life to Advanced Age. Portrait. 8vo. **16s.**

———— Voyages of Discovery and Research within the Arctic Regions, from 1818 to the present time. Abridged and arranged from the Official Narratives. 8vo. 15s.

———— (SIR GEORGE) Ceylon; Past and Present. Map. Post 8vo. 6s. 6d.

———— (JOHN) Naval Worthies of Queen Elizabeth's Reign, their Gallant Deeds, Daring Adventures, and Services in the infant state of the British Navy. 8vo. 14s.

———— Life and Voyages of Sir Francis Drake. With numerous Original Letters. Post 8vo. 2s. 6d.

BEES AND FLOWERS. Two Essays. By Rev. Thomas James. Reprinted from the "Quarterly Review." Fcap. 8vo. 1s. each.

BELL'S (SIR CHARLES) Mechanism and Vital Endowments of the Hand as evincing Design. *Sixth Edition.* Woodcuts. Post 8vo. 7s. 6d.

BENEDICT'S (JULES) Sketch of the Life and Works of Felix Mendelssohn Bartholdy. *Second Edition.* 8vo. 2s. 6d.

BERTHA'S Journal during a Visit to her Uncle in England. Containing a Variety of Interesting and Instructive Information. *Seventh Edition.* Woodcuts. 12mo. 7s. 6d.

BIRCH'S (SAMUEL) History of Ancient Pottery and Porcelain: Egyptian, Assyrian, Greek, Roman, and Etruscan. With 200 Illustra- 2 Vols. Medium 8vo. 42s.

BLUNT'S (REV. J. J.) Principles for the proper understanding of the Mosaic Writings, stated and applied, together with an Incidental Argument for the truth of the Resurrection of our Lord. Being the tions. HULSEAN LECTURES for 1832. Post 8vo. 6s. 6d.

———— Undesigned Coincidences in the Writings of the Old and New Testament, an Argument of their Veracity: with an Appendix containing Undesigned Coincidences between the Gospels Acts, and Josephus. *Sixth Edition.* Post 8vo. 7s. 6d.

———— History of the Church in the First Three Centuries. *Second Edition.* 8vo. 9s. 6d.

———— Parish Priest; His Duties, Acquirements and Obligations. *Third Edition.* Post 8vo. 7s. 6d.

———— Lectures on the Right Use of the Early Fathers. *Second Edition.* 8vo. 15s.

———— Plain Sermons Preached to a Country Congregation. *Second Edition.* 2 Vols. Post 8vo. 7s. 6d. each

BLACKSTONE'S COMMENTARIES on the Laws of England. A
New Edition, adapted to the present state of the law. By R. MALCOLM
KERR, LL.D. 4 Vols. 8vo. 42s.

——————— FOR STUDENTS. Being those Portions of the above work which relate to the BRITISH CONSTITUTION
and the RIGHTS OF PERSONS. By R. MALCOLM KERR, LLD. *Second Thousand*. Post 8vo. 9s.

BLAINE (ROBERTON) on the Laws of Artistic Copyright and their
Defects, for Artists, Engravers, Printsellers, &c. 8vo. 3s. 6d.

BOOK OF COMMON PRAYER. With 1000 Illustrations of
Borders, Initials, and Woodcut Vignettes. *A New Edition.* Medium
8vo. 21s. **cloth, 31s.** 6d. *calf,* or 42s. *morocco.*

BOSWELL'S (JAMES) Life of Dr. Johnson. Including the Tour to
the Hebrides. Edited by Mr. CROKER. *Third Edition.* Portraits. Royal
8vo. 10s. sewed, 12s. cloth.

BORROW'S (GEORGE) Lavengro; The Scholar—The **Gipsy—and**
the **Priest.** Portrait. 3 Vols. Post 8vo. 30s.

——————— Romany Rye; a Sequel to Lavengro. *Second
Edition.* 2 Vols. **Post 8vo. 21s.**

——————— Bible in **Spain; or the** Journeys, Adventures, and
Imprisonments **of an Englishman** in an Attempt to circulate the
Scriptures in the **Peninsula. 3 Vols.** Post 8vo. 27s., or *Popular Edition.*
16mo, 6s.

——————— Zincali, **or the Gipsies of Spain;** their Manners,
Customs, Religion, and Language. 2 **Vols.** Post 8vo. 18s., or *Popular
Edition.* 16mo, 6s.

BRAY'S (MRS.) Life of Thomas Stothard, **R.A.** With Personal
Reminiscences. Illustrated with Portrait **and 60** Woodcuts of his
chief works. 4to.

BREWSTER'S (SIR DAVID) Martyrs of Science, or the Lives of
Galileo, Tycho Brahe, and Kepler. *Fourth Edition.* Fcap. 8vo. 4s. 6d.

——————— More **Worlds** than One. The Creed **of the Philo-**
sopher and the Hope of the Christian. *Eighth Edition.* **Post 8vo. 6s.**

——————— Stereoscope: its History, **Theory, Construction,**
and Application to the Arts and **to** Education. **Woodcuts. 12mo.**
5s. 6d.

——————— Kaleidoscope: its **History, Theory, and** Construction,
with **its** application to **the Fine and Useful Arts.** *Second Edition.*
Woodcuts. Post 8vo. 5s. 6d.

BRITISH **ASSOCIATION** REPORTS. 8vo. **York and** Oxford,
1831-32, 13s. 6d. Cambridge, **1833, 12s.** Edinburgh, 1834, 15s. Dublin,
1835, 13s. 6d. Bristol, 1836, 12s. Liverpool, 1837, 16s. 6d. Newcastle,
1838, 15s. Birmingham, 1839, 13s. 6d. Glasgow, 1840, 15s. Plymouth,
1841, 13s. 6d. Manchester, 1842, 10s. 6d. Cork, 1843, 12s. York, 1844.
20s. Cambridge, 1845, 12s. Southampton, 1846, 15s. Oxford, 1847, 18s.
Swansea, 1848, 9s. Birmingham, 1849, 10s. Edinburgh, 1850, 15s. Ipswich,
1851, 16s. 6d. Belfast, 1852, 15s. Hull, 1853, 10s. 6d. Liverpool, 1854, 18s.
Glasgow, 1855, 15s.; Cheltenham, 1856, 18s; Dublin, 1857, 15s; Leeds,
1858, 20s.

BRITISH CLASSICS. A New Series of Standard English
Authors, printed from the most correct text, and edited with elucidatory notes. Published occasionally in demy 8vo. Volumes.

Already Published.

GOLDSMITH'S WORKS. Edited by PETER CUNNINGHAM, F.S.A.
Vignettes. 4 Vols. 20s.

GIBBON'S DECLINE AND FALL OF THE ROMAN EMPIRE.
Edited by WILLIAM SMITH, LL.D. Portrait and Maps. 8 Vols. 60s.

JOHNSON'S LIVES OF THE ENGLISH POETS. Edited by PETER
CUNNINGHAM, F.S.A. 3 Vols. 22s. 6d.

BYRON'S POETICAL WORKS. Edited, with Notes. 6 vols. 45s.

In Preparation.

WORKS OF POPE. Edited, with Notes.
WORKS OF DRYDEN. Edited, with Notes.
HUME'S HISTORY OF ENGLAND. Edited, with Notes.
LIFE, LETTERS, AND JOURNALS OF SWIFT. By JOHN FORSTER.
WORKS OF SWIFT. Edited by JOHN FORSTER.

BROUGHTON'S (LORD) Journey through Albania and other
Provinces of Turkey in Europe and Asia, to Constantinople, 1809—10.
Third Edition. Maps and Woodcuts. 2 Vols. 8vo. 30s.

———————— Visits to Italy, from the Year 1816 to 1824.
Second Edition. 2 vols. Post 8vo. 18s.

BUBBLES FROM THE BRUNNEN OF NASSAU. By an Old
MAN. *Sixth Edition.* 16mo. 5s.

BUNBURY'S (C. J. F.) Journal of a Residence at the Cape of Good
Hope; with Excursions into the Interior, and Notes on the Natural
History and Native Tribes of the Country. Woodcuts. Post 8vo. 9s.

BUNYAN (JOHN) and Oliver Cromwell. Select Biographies. By
ROBERT SOUTHEY. Post 8vo. 2s. 6d.

BUONAPARTE'S (NAPOLEON) Confidential Correspondence with his
Brother Joseph, sometime King of Spain. *Second Edition.* 2 vols. 8vo.
26s.

BURGHERSH'S (LORD) Memoir of the Operations of the Allied
Armies under Prince Schwarzenberg and Marshal Blucher during the
latter end of 1813—14. 8vo. 21s.

———————— Early Campaigns of the Duke of Wellington in
Portugal and Spain. 8vo. 8s. 6d.

BURGON'S (Rev. J. W.) Portrait of a Christian Gentleman: a
Memoir of the late Patrick Fraser Tytler, author of "The History of
Scotland." *Second Edition.* Post 8vo. 9s.

BURN'S (LIEUT-COL.) French and English Dictionary of Naval
and Military Technical Terms. *Third Edition.* Crown 8vo. 15s.

BURNS' (ROBERT) Life. By JOHN GIBSON LOCKHART. Fifth
Edition. Fcap. 8vo. 3s.

BURR'S (G. D.) Instructions in Practical Surveying, Topographical Plan Drawing, and on sketching ground without Instruments.
Third Edition. Woodcuts. Post 8vo. 7s. 6d.

BUXTON'S (Sir Fowell) Memoirs. With Selections from his Correspondence. By his Son. Portrait. *Fifth Edition.* 8vo. 16s. The same, Post 8vo. 8s. 6d.; or, an *Abridged Edition,* Portrait, Fcap. 8vo. 2s.

BYRON'S (Lord) Life, Letters, and Journals. By Thomas Moore. Plates. 6 Vols. Fcap. 8vo. 18s.

———— Life, Letters, and Journals. By Thomas Moore. With Portraits. Royal 8vo. 9s., or 10s. 6d. in cloth.

———— Poetical Works. Portrait. 6 Vols. Demy 8vo. 45s.

———— Poetical Works. Plates. 10 Vols. Fcap. 8vo. 30s.

———— Poetical Works. With Engravings. Royal 8vo. 9s., or 10s. 6d. in cloth.

———— Poetical Works. Printed in small but beautifully clear type. Portrait. Crown 8vo. 9s.

———— Poetical Works. 8 Vols. 24mo. 20s.

———— Childe Harold's Pilgrimage. Illustrated, with 80 Wood Engravings. Crown 8vo. 21s.

———— Childe Harold. Crown 8vo. 10s. 6d.

———— Childe Harold. 24mo. 2s. 6d.

———— Childe Harold. Portrait and Titles. Fcap. 8vo. 1s.

———— Childe Harold. Portrait. Post 8vo. 6d.

———— Dramas. 2 Vols. 24mo. 5s.

———— Tales and Poems. 24mo. 2s. 6d.

———— Miscellaneous. 2 Vols. 24mo. 5s.

———— Don Juan and Beppo. 2 Vols. 24mo. 5s.

———— Beauties. Poetry and Prose. Portrait, Fcap. 8vo. 3s. 6d.

CARNARVON'S (Lord) Portugal, Gallicia, and the Basque Provinces. From Notes made during a Journey to those Countries. *Third Edition.* Post 8vo. 6s.

———— Archæology of Berkshire. Fcap. 8vo. 1s.

CAMPBELL'S (Lord) Lives of the Lord Chancellors and Keepers of the Great Seal of England. From the Earliest Times to the Death of Lord Eldon in 1838. *Fourth Edition.* 10 Vols. Crown 8vo. 6s. each.

———— Life of Lord Chancellor Bacon. Fcap. 8vo. 2s. 6d.

———— Lives of the Chief Justices of England. From the Norman Conquest to the Death of Lord Tenterden. *Second Edition.* 3 Vols. 8vo. 42s.

———— Shakspeare's Legal Acquirements Considered. 8vo. 5s. 6d.

———— (George) Modern India. A Sketch of the System of Civil Government. With some Account of the Natives and Native Institutions. *Second Edition.* 8vo. 16s.

———— India as it may be. An Outline of a proposed Government and Policy. 8vo. 12s.

———— (Thos.) Short Lives of the British Poets. With an Essay on English Poetry. Post 8vo. 6s.

8   LIST OF WORKS

CALVIN'S (John) **Life.** With Extracts from his Correspondence
By Thomas H. Dyer. Portrait. 8vo. 15s.

CALLCOTT'S (Lady) Little Arthur's History of England.
Nineteenth Edition. With 20 Woodcuts. Fcap. 8vo. 2s. 6d.

CARMICHAEL'S (A. N.) Greek Verbs. Their Formations,
Irregularities, and Defects. *Second Edition.* **Post 8vo. 8s. 6d.**

CASTLEREAGH (The) DESPATCHES, from the commencement
of the official career of the late Viscount Castlereagh to the close of his
life. Edited by the Marquis of Londonderry. 12 Vols. 8vo. 14s. each.

CATHCART'S (Sir George) Commentaries on the **War in Russia**
and Germany, 1812-13. Plans. 8vo. 14s.

———— Military Operations in Kaffraria, which **led to the**
Termination of the Kaffir **War.** *Second Edition.* 8vo. 12s.

CAVALCASELLE (G. B.) Notices of the Early Flemish Painters;
Their Lives and **Works.** Woodcuts. Post 8vo. 12s.

CHANTREY (Sir Francis). Winged Words on Chantrey's Wood-
cocks. Edited by Jas. P. Muirhead. Etchings. Square 8vo. 10s. 6d.

CHARMED ROE (The) ; or, The Story of the Little Brother and
Sister. By Otto Speckter. Plates. 16mo. 5s.

COBBOLD'S (Rev. R. H.) Pictures of the Chinese drawn by themselves. With Descriptions. Plates. Crown 8vo. 9s.

CLAUSEWITZ'S (Carl Von) Campaign of 1812, in **Russia.**
Translated from the German by Lord Ellesmere. Map. 8vo. 10s. 6d.

CLIVE'S (Lord) Life. By Rev. G. R. Gleig, M.A. Post 8vo. 6s.

COLERIDGE (Samuel Taylor). Specimens of his Table-Talk.
Fourth Edition. Portrait. Fcap. 8vo. 6s.

———— (Henry Nelson) Introductions to the Study of
the Greek Classic Poets. *Third Edition.* Fcap. 8vo. 5s. 6d.

COLONIAL **LIBRARY.** [See Home and Colonial Library.]

COOKERY (Domestic). Founded on Principles of Economy and
Practical Knowledge, and adapted for Private Families. *New Edition.*
Woodcuts. Fcap. 8vo. **5s.**

CORNWALLIS (The) Papers and Correspondence during the
American War,—Administrations in India,—Union with Ireland, and
Peace of Amiens. Edited by Charles Ross. *Second Edition.* 3 Vols.
8vo. 63s.

CRABBE'S (Rev. George) Life, Letters, and Journals. By his Son.
Portrait. Fcap. 8vo. 3s.

———— Poetical Works. Plates. 8 Vols. Fcap. 8vo. 24s.

———— Poetical Works. Plates. Royal 8vo. 10s. 6d.

CRAIK'S (G. L.) Pursuit of Knowledge under Difficulties.
New Edition. 2 Vols. Post 8vo. 12s.

CURZON'S (Hon. Robert) Visits to the Monasteries of the Levant.
Fourth Edition. Woodcuts. Post 8vo. 15s.

———— Armenia and Erzeroum. A Year on the Frontiers of
Russia, Turkey, and Persia. *Third Edition.* Woodcuts. Post 8vo. 7s. 6d.

CUNNINGHAM'S (ALLAN) **Life of** Sir David Wilkie. With his Journals and Critical Remarks on Works of Art. Portrait. 3 Vols. 8vo. 42s.

———————— Poems and Songs. Now first collected and arranged, with Biographical Notice. 24mo 2s. 6d.

———————— (CAPT. J. D.) History of **the** Sikhs. From the Origin of the Nation to the Battle **of the Sutlej.** *Second Edition* Maps. 8vo. 15s.

———————— (PETER) London—Past and Present. **A** Handbook to the Antiquities, Curiosities, Churches, Works of Art, Public Buildings, and Places connected with interesting and historical associations. *Second Edition.* Post 8vo. 16s.

———————— Modern London. **A** complete Guide **for** Visitors to the Metropolis. Map. 16mo. **5s.**

———————— Westminster Abbey. Its Art, Architecture, **and** Associations. Woodcuts. Fcap. 8vo. 1s.

———————— Works of Oliver Goldsmith. Edited **with** Notes. Vignettes. **4 vols.** 8vo. 30s. (Murray's British Classics.)

———————— Lives of Eminent English Poets. By SAMUEL JOHNSON, LL.D. Edited with Notes. 3 vols. 8vo. 22s. 6d. (Murray's British Classics.)

CROKER'S (J. W.) **Progressive Geography** for Children. *Fifth Edition.* 18mo. 1s. 6d.

———————— Stories **for Children, Selected** from the History **of** England. *Fifteenth Edition.* Woodcuts. 16mo. 2s. 6d.

———————— Boswell's **Life of Johnson.** Including the Tour to the Hebrides. *Third Edition.* Portraits. Royal 8vo. 10s. sewed, or 12s. cloth.

———————— LORD HERVEY's Memoirs of· the Reign of George the Second, from his Accession to **the death of** Queen Caroline. Edited with Notes. *Second Edition.* Portrait. 2 Vols. 8vo. 21s.

———————— Essays on the Early Period of the French Revolution. Reprinted from the Quarterly Review. 8vo. 15s.

———————— Historical Essay on the Guillotine. Fcap. 8vo. 1s.

CROMWELL (OLIVER) **and** John Bunyan. By ROBERT SOUTHEY. Post 8vo. 2s. 6d.

CROWE'S (J. A.) **Notices of** the Early Flemish **Painters; their** Lives and Works. Woodcuts. Post 8vo. 12s.

CURETON (REV. W.) Remains of a very Ancient **Recension of** the Four Gospels in Syriac, hitherto unknown **in Europe. Discovered,** Edited, and Translated. 4to. 21s.

DARWIN'S (CHARLES) Journal of Researches into the Natural History **and** Geology of the Countries visited during **a** Voyage round the World. Post 8vo. 8s. 6d.

———————— Origin of Species by Means of Natural Selection; or, **the** Preservation of Favoured Races in the Struggle for Life. Post 8vo. **14s.**

DAVIS'S (SIR **J. F.**) China: **A General** Description of that Empire and its Inhabitants, down **to 1857.** *New Edition.* Woodcuts. 2 Vols. Post 8vo. **14s.**

DAVY'S (SIR HUMPHRY) Consolations in Travel; or, **Last Days** of a Philosopher. *Fifth Edition.* Woodcuts. Fcap. 8vo. 6s.

———————— Salmonia; or, Days of Fly Fishing. With some Account of the Habits **of** Fishes belonging **to** the genus Salmo. *Fourth Edition.* Woodcuts. Fcap. 8vo. 6s.

DENNIS' (George) Cities and Cemeteries of Etruria. Plates. 2 Vols. 8vo. 42s.

DOG-BREAKING; the Most Expeditious, Certain, and Easy Method, whether great excellence or only mediocrity be required. By LIEUT.-COL. HUTCHINSON. *Third Edition.* Revised and enlarged. Woodcuts. Post 8vo. 9s.

DOMESTIC MODERN COOKERY. Founded on Principles of Economy and Practical Knowledge, and adapted for Private Families. *New Edition.* Woodcuts. Fcap. 8vo. 5s.

DOUGLAS'S (General Sir Howard) Treatise on the Theory and Practice of Gunnery. *Fourth Edition.* Plates. 8vo. 21s.

———— Treatise on Military Bridges, and the Passages of Rivers in Military Operations. *Third Edition.* Plates. 8vo. 21s.

———— Naval Warfare with Steam. 8vo. 8s. 6d.

———— Modern Systems of Fortification, with special reference to the Naval, Littoral, and Internal Defence of England. Plans. 8vo. 12s.

DRAKE'S (Sir Francis) Life, Voyages, and Exploits, by Sea and Land. By JOHN BARROW. *Third Edition.* Post 8vo. 2s. 6d.

DRINKWATER'S (John) History of the Siege of Gibraltar, 1779-1783. With a Description and Account of that Garrison from the Earliest Periods. Post 8vo. 2s. 6d.

DUDLEY'S (Earl of) Letters to the late Bishop of Llandaff. *Second Edition.* Portrait. 8vo. 10s. 6d.

DUFFERIN'S (Lord) Letters from High Latitudes, being some Account of a Yacht Voyage to Iceland, &c., in 1856. *Fourth Edition.* Woodcuts. Post 8vo. 9s.

DURHAM'S (Admiral Sir Philip) Naval Life and Services. By CAPT. ALEXANDER MURRAY. 8vo. 5s. 6d.

DYER'S (Thomas H.) Life and Letters of John Calvin. Compiled from authentic Sources. Portrait. 8vo. 15s.

EASTLAKE (Sir Charles) The Schools of Painting in Italy. From the Earliest times. From the German of KUGLER. Edited, with Notes. *Third Edition.* Illustrated from the Old Masters. 2 Vols. Post 8vo. 30s.

EASTWICK'S (E. B.) Handbook for Bombay and Madras, with Directions for Travellers, Officers, &c. Map. 2 Vols. Post 8vo. 24s.

EDWARDS' (W. H.) Voyage up the River Amazon, including a Visit to Para. Post 8vo. 2s. 6d.

EGERTON'S (Hon. Capt. Francis) Journal of a Winter's Tour in India; with a Visit to Nepaul. Woodcuts. 2 Vols. Post 8vo. 18s.

ELDON'S (Lord Chancellor) Public and Private Life, with Selections from his Correspondence and Diaries. By HORACE TWISS. *Third Edition.* Portrait. 2 Vols. Post 8vo. 21s.

ELIOT'S (Hon. W. G. C.) Khans of the Crimea. Being a Narrative of an Embassy from Frederick the Great to the Court of Krim Gerai. Translated from the German. Post 8vo. 6s.

ELLIS (Mrs.) On the Education of Character, with Hints on Moral Training. Post 8vo. 7s. 6d.

———— (Rev. W.) Three Visits to Madagascar. During 1853, '54, and '56, including a Journey to the Capital, with notices of Natural History, and Present Civilisation of the People. *Fifth Thousand.* Map and Woodcuts. 8vo. 16s.

ELLESMERE'S (LORD) Two Sieges of Vienna by the Turks.
Translated from the German. Post 8vo. 2s. 6d.

———— - Second Campaign of Radetzky in Piedmont.
The Defence of Temeswár and the Camp of the Ban. From the German.
Post 8vo. 6s. 6d.

———— Campaign of 1812 in Russia, from the German
of General Carl Von Clausewitz. Map. 8vo. 10s. 6d.

———— Pilgrimage, and other Poems. Crown 4to. 24s.

———— Essays on History, Biography, Geography, and
Engineering. 8vo. 12s.

ELPHINSTONE'S (HON. MOUNTSTUART) History of India—the
Hindoo and Mahomedan Periods. Fourth Edition. With an Index.
Map. 8vo. 18s.

ELWIN'S (REV. W.) Lives of Eminent British Poets. From
Chaucer to Wordsworth. 4 Vols. 8vo. In Preparation.

ENGLAND (HISTORY OF) from the Peace of Utrecht to the Peace
of Versailles, 1713—83. By LORD MAHON. Library Edition, 7 Vols.
8vo, 93s.; or, Popular Edition, 7 Vols. Post 8vo. 35s.

———— From the First Invasion by the Romans,
down to the 14th year of Queen Victoria's Reign. By MRS. MARKHAM.
98th Edition. Woodcuts. 12mo. 6s.

———— As IT IS: Social, Political, and Industrial, in the
19th Century. By W. JOHNSTON. 2 Vols. Post 8vo. 18s.

———— and France under the House of Lancaster. With an
Introductory View of the Early Reformation. Second Edition. 8vo. 15s.

ENGLISHWOMAN IN AMERICA. Post 8vo. 10s. 6d.

———— RUSSIA: or, Impressions of Manners
and Society during a Ten Years' Residence in that Country. Fifth
Thousand. Woodcuts. Post 8vo. 10s. 6d.

EOTHEN; or, Traces of Travel brought Home from the East.
A New Edition. Post 8vo. 7s. 6d.

ERSKINE'S (CAPT., R.N.) Journal of a Cruise among the Islands
of the Western Pacific, including the Fejees, and others inhabited by
the Polynesian Negro Races. Plates. 8vo. 16s.

ESKIMAUX (THE) and English Vocabulary, for the use of Travellers
in the Arctic Regions. 16mo. 3s. 6d.

ESSAYS FROM "THE TIMES." Being a Selection from the
LITERARY PAPERS which have appeared in that Journal. Seventh
Thousand. 2 vols. Fcap. 8vo. 8s.

EXETER'S (BISHOP OF) Letters to the late Charles Butler, on the
Theological parts of his Book of the Roman Catholic Church; with
Remarks on certain Works of Dr Milner and Dr. Lingard, and on some
parts of the Evidence of Dr. Doyle. Second Edition. 8vo. 16s.

FAIRY RING (THE), A Collection of TALES and STORIES for Young
Persons. From the German. By J. E. TAYLOR. Illustrated by RICHARD
DOYLE. Second Edition. Fcap. 8vo.

FALKNER'S (FRED.) Muck Manual for the Use of Farmers. A
Treatise on the Nature and Value of Manures. Second Edition, with a
Glossary of Terms and an Index. Fcap. 8vo. 5s.

FAMILY RECEIPT-BOOK. A Collection of a Thousand Valuable and Useful Receipts. Fcap. 8vo. 5s. 6d.

FANCOURT'S (Col.) History of Yucatan, from its Discovery to the Close of the 17th Century. With Map. 8vo. 10s 6d.

FARRAR'S (Rev. A. S.) Science in Theology. Sermons Preached before the University of Oxford. 8vo. 9s.

FEATHERSTONHAUGH'S (G. W.) Tour through the Slave States of North America, from the River Potomac, to Texas and the Frontiers of Mexico. Plates. 2 Vols. 8vo. 26s.

FELLOWS' (Sir Charles) Travels and Researches in Asia Minor, more particularly in the Province of Lydia. New Edition. Plates. Post 8vo. 9s.

FERGUSSON'S (James) Palaces of Nineveh and Persepolis Restored: an Essay on Ancient Assyrian and Persian Architecture. With 45 Woodcuts. 8vo. 16s.

———————— Handbook of Architecture. Being a Concise and Popular Account of the Different Styles prevailing in all Ages and Countries in the World. With a Description of the most remarkable Buildings. Fourth Thousand. With 850 Illustrations. 8vo. 26s.

FERRIER'S (T. P.) Caravan Journeys in Persia, Affghanistan, Herat, Turkistan, and Beloochistan, with Descriptions of Meshed, Balk, and Candahar, and Sketches of the Nomade Tribes of Central Asia. Second Edition. Map. 8vo. 21s.

———————— History of the Afghans. Map. 8vo. 21s.

FEUERBACH'S Remarkable German Crimes and Trials. Translated from the German by Lady Duff Gordon. 8vo. 12s.

FISHER'S (Rev. George) Elements of Geometry, for the Use of Schools. Fifth Edition. 18mo. 1s. 6d.

———————— First Principles of Algebra, for the Use of Schools. Fifth Edition. 18mo. 1s. 6d.

FLOWER GARDEN (The). An Essay. By Rev. Thos. James. Reprinted from the "Quarterly Review." Fcap. 8vo. 1s.

FORD'S (Richard) Handbook for Spain, Andalusia, Ronda, Valencia, Catalonia, Granada, Gallicia, Arragon, Navarre, &c. Third Edition. 2 Vols. Post 8vo. 30s.

———————— Gatherings from Spain. Post 8vo. 6s.

FORSTER'S (John) Historical & Biographical Essays. 2 Vols. Post 8vo. 21s.
I. The Grand Remonstrance, 1641.
II. The Plantagenets and the Tudors.
III. Civil Wars & Oliver Cromwell.
IV. Daniel De Foe.
V. Sir Richard Steele.
VI. Charles Churchill.
VII. Samuel Foote.

FORSYTH'S (William) Hortensius, or the Advocate: an Historical Essay on the Office and Duties of an Advocate. Post 8vo. 12s.

———————— History of Napoleon at St. Helena. From the Letters and Journals of Sir Hudson Lowe. Portrait and Maps. 3 Vols. 8vo. 45s.

FORTUNE'S (Robert) Narrative of Two Visits to China, between the years 1843-52, with full Descriptions of the Culture of the Tea Plant. Third Edition. Woodcuts. 2 Vols. Post 8vo. 18s.

———————— Residence among the Chinese: Inland, on the Coast, and at Sea, during 1853-56. Woodcuts. 8vo. 16s.

FRANCE (History of). From the Conquest by the Gauls to the Death of Louis Philippe. By Mrs. Markham. 56th Thousand. Woodcuts. 12mo. 6s.

FRENCH (THE) in Algiers; The Soldier of the Foreign Legion—
and the Prisoners of Abd-el-Kadir. Translated by Lady DUFF GORDON.
Post 8vo. 2s. 6d.

GALTON'S (FRANCIS) Art of Travel; or, Hints on the Shifts and
Contrivances available in Wild Countries. *Third Edition, enlarged.*
Woodcuts. Post 8vo. 7s. 6d.

GEOGRAPHICAL (THE) Journal. Published by the Royal Geographical Society of London. 8vo.

GERMANY (HISTORY OF). From the Invasion by Marius, to the
present time. On the plan of Mrs. MARKHAM. *Fifteenth Thousand.* Woodcuts. 12mo. 6s.

GIBBON'S (EDWARD) Decline and Fall of the Roman Empire. A
New Edition. Preceded by his Autobiography. Edited with Notes
by Dr. WM. SMITH. Maps. 8 Vols. 8vo. 60s.

———————— The Student's Gibbon; Being the History of the
Decline and Fall. Abridged, Incorporating the Researches of Recent
Commentators. By Dr. WM. SMITH. *Sixth Thousand.* Woodcuts. Post
8vo. 7s. 6d.

GIFFARD'S (EDWARD) Deeds of Naval Daring; or, Anecdotes of
the British Navy. 2 Vols. Fcap. 8vo. 5s.

GISBORNE'S (THOMAS) Essays on Agriculture. *Third Edition.*
Post 8vo.

GLADSTONE'S (W. E.) Prayers arranged from the Liturgy for
Family Use. *Second Edition.* 12mo. 2s. 6d.

GOLDSMITH'S (OLIVER) Works. A New Edition. Printed from
the last editions revised by the Author. Edited by PETER CUNNING-
HAM. Vignettes. 4 Vols. 8vo. 30s. (Murray's British Classics.)

GLEIG'S (REV. G. R.) Campaigns of the British Army at Washington and New Orleans. Post 8vo. 2s. 6d.

———————— Story of the Battle of Waterloo. Compiled from Public
and Authentic Sources. Post 8vo. 5s.

———————— Narrative of Sir Robert Sale's Brigade in Afghanistan,
with an Account of the Seizure and Defence of Jellalabad. Post 8vo. 2s. 6d.

———————— Life of Robert Lord Clive. Post 8vo. 5s.

———————— Life and Letters of General Sir Thomas Munro. Post
8vo. 5s.

GORDON'S (SIR ALEX. DUFF) Sketches of German Life, and Scenes
from the War of Liberation. From the German. Post 8vo. 6s.

———————— (LADY DUFF) Amber-Witch: the most interesting
Trial for Witchcraft ever known. From the German. Post 8vo. 2s. 6d.

———————— French in Algiers. 1. The Soldier of the Foreign
Legion. 2. The Prisoners of Abd-el-Kadir. From the French.
Post 8vo. 2s. 6d.

———————— Remarkable German Crimes and Trials. From the
German of Fuerbach. 8vo. 12s.

GRANT'S (ASAHEL) Nestorians, or the Lost Tribes; containing
Evidence of their Identity, their Manners, Customs, and Ceremonies;
with Sketches of Travel in Ancient Assyria, Armenia, and Mesopotamia;
and Illustrations of Scripture Prophecy. *Third Edition.* Fcap 8vo. 6s.

GRENVILLE (THE) PAPERS. Being the Public and Private
Correspondence of George Grenville, his Friends and Contemporaries,
during a period of 30 years.—Including his DIARY OF POLITICAL
EVENTS while First Lord of the Treasury. Edited, with Notes, by
W. J. SMITH. 4 Vols. 8vo. 16s. each.

GREEK GRAMMAR FOR SCHOOLS. Abridged from Matthiæ.
By the BISHOP OF LONDON. *Ninth Edition*, revised by Rev. J. EDWARDS.
12mo. 3s.

GREY'S (SIR GEORGE) Polynesian Mythology, and Ancient
Traditional History of the New Zealand Race. Woodcuts. Post
8vo. 10s. 6d.

GROTE'S (GEORGE) History of Greece. From the Earliest Times
to the close of the generation contemporary with the death of Alexander
the Great. *Third Edition.* Maps and Index. 12 vols. 8vo. 16s. each.

———— (MRS.) Memoir of the Life of the late Ary Scheffer.
Portrait, 8vo. (Nearly Ready.)

GROSVENOR'S (LORD ROBERT) Leaves from my Journal during
the Summer of 1851. *Second Edition.* Plates. Post 8vo. 3s. 6d.

GUSTAVUS VASA (History of), King of Sweden. With Extracts
from his Correspondence. Portrait. 8vo. 10s. 6d.

HALLAM'S (HENRY) Constitutional History of England, from the
Accession of Henry the Seventh to the Death of George the Second.
Seventh Edition. 3 Vols. 8vo. 30s.

———— History of Europe during the Middle Ages.
Tenth Edition. 3 Vols. 8vo. 30s.

———— Introduction to the Literary History of Europe, during
the 16th, 17th, and 18th Centuries. *Fourth Edition.* 3 Vols. 8vo. 36s.

———— Literary Essays and Characters. Selected from the
last work. Fcap. 8vo. 2s.

———— Historical Works. Containing the History of England,—The Middle Ages of Europe,—and the Literary History of
Europe. *Complete Edition.* 10 Vols. Post 8vo. 6s. each.

HAMILTON'S (JAMES) Wanderings in Northern Africa, Benghazi,
Cyrene, the Oasis of Siwah, &c. *Second Edition.* Woodcuts. Post 8vo. 12s.

———— (WALTER) Hindostan, Geographically, Statistically,
and Historically. Map. 2 Vols. 4to. 94s. 6d.

HAMPDEN'S (BISHOP) Essay on the Philosophical Evidence of
Christianity, or the Credibility obtained to a Scripture Revelation
from its Coincidence with the Facts of Nature. 8vo. 9s. 6d.

HARCOURT'S (EDWARD VERNON) Sketch of Madeira ; with Map
and Plates. Post 8vo. 8s. 6d.

HART'S ARMY LIST. (*Quarterly and Annually.*) 8vo.

HAY'S (J. H. DRUMMOND) Western Barbary, its wild Tribes and
savage Animals. Post 8vo. 2s. 6d.

HEBER (BISHOP) Parish Sermons ; on the Lessons, the Gospel,
or the Epistle, for every Sunday in the Year, and for Week-day Festivals.
Sixth Edition. 2 Vols. Post 8vo. 16s.

———— Sermons Preached in England. *Second Edition.* 8vo. 9s. 6d.

———— Hymns written and adapted for the Weekly Church
Service of the Year. *Twelfth Edition.* 16mo. 2s.

———— Poetical Works. *Fifth Edition.* Portrait. Fcap. 8vo.
7s. 6d.

———— Journey through the Upper Provinces of India, From
Calcutta to Bombay, with a Journey to Madras and the Southern Provinces. 2 Vols. Post 8vo. 12s.

HAND-BOOK OF TRAVEL-TALK; or, Conversations in English, German, French, and Italian. 18mo. 3s. 6d.

———— NORTH GERMANY—HOLLAND, BELGIUM, and the Rhine to Switzerland. Map. Post 8vo. 10s.

———— SOUTH GERMANY—Bavaria, Austria, Salzberg, the Austrian and Bavarian Alps, the Tyrol, and the Danube, from Ulm to the Black Sea. Map. Post 8vo. 10s.

———— PAINTING—the German, Flemish, and Dutch Schools. From the German of KUGLER. A New Edition. Edited by DR. WAAGEN. Woodcuts. Post 8vo. (In the Press.)

———— SWITZERLAND—the Alps of Savoy, and Piedmont. Maps. Post 8vo. 9s.

———— FRANCE—Normandy, Brittany, the French Alps, the Rivers Loire, Seine, Rhone, and Garonne, Dauphiné, Provence, and the Pyrenees. Maps. Post 8vo. 10s.

———— SPAIN—Andalusia, Ronda, Granada, Valencia, Catalonia, Gallicia, Arragon, and Navarre. Maps. 2 Vols. Post 8vo. 30s.

———— PORTUGAL, LISBON, &c. Map. Post 8vo. 9s.

———— PAINTING—SPANISH AND FRENCH SCHOOLS. By SIR EDMUND HEAD, BART. Woodcuts. Post 8vo. 12s.

———— NORTH ITALY—Florence, Sardinia, Genoa, the Riviera, Venice, Lombardy, and Tuscany. Map. Post 8vo. 2 Vols. 12s.

———— CENTRAL ITALY—SOUTH TUSCANY and the PAPAL STATES. Map. Post 8vo. 7s.

———— ROME—AND ITS ENVIRONS. Map. Post 8vo. 9s.

———— SOUTH ITALY—Naples, Pompeii, Herculaneum, Vesuvius, &c. Map. Post 8vo. 10s.

———— SICILY. Map. Post 8vo. (In the Press.)

———— PAINTING—the Italian Schools. From the German of KUGLER. Edited by Sir CHARLES EASTLAKE, R. A. Woodcuts. 2 Vols. Post 8vo. 30s.

———— EARLY ITALIAN PAINTERS AND PROGRESS OF PAINTING IN ITALY. By Mrs. JAMESON. Woodcuts. Post 8vo. 12s.

———— BIOGRAPHICAL DICTIONARY OF ITALIAN PAINTERS. With a Chart. Post 8vo. 6s. 6d.

———— GREECE—the Ionian Islands, Albania, Thessaly, and Macedonia. Maps. Post 8vo. 15s.

———— TURKEY—MALTA, ASIA MINOR, CONSTANTINOPLE, Armenia, Mesopotamia, &c. Maps. Post 8vo.

———— EGYPT—Thebes, the Nile, Alexandria, Cairo, the Pyramids, Mount Sinai, &c. Map. Post 8vo. 15s.

———— SYRIA AND PALESTINE; the Peninsula of Sinai, Edom, and the Syrian Desert. Maps. 2 Vols. Post 8vo. 24s.

———— BOMBAY AND MADRAS. Map. 2 Vols. Post 8vo. 24s.

———— DENMARK—NORWAY and SWEDEN. Maps. Post 8vo. 15s.

———— RUSSIA—THE BALTIC AND FINLAND. Maps. Post 8vo. 12s.

HANDBOOK OF LONDON, Past and Present. Alphabetically arranged. *Second Edition.* Post 8vo. 16s.

———— MODERN LONDON. A Guide to all objects of interest in the Metropolis. Map. 16mo. 5s.

———— ENVIRONS OF LONDON. Including a Circle of 30 Miles round St. Paul's. Maps. Post 8vo. (*In preparation.*)

———— DEVON AND CORNWALL. Maps. Post 8vo. 7s. 6d.

———— WILTS, DORSET, AND SOMERSET. Map. Post 8vo. 7s. 6d.

———— KENT AND SUSSEX. Map. Post 8vo. 10s.

———— SURREY, HANTS, and the Isle of Wight. Maps. Post 8vo. 7s. 6d.

———— WESTMINSTER ABBEY—its Art, Architecture, and Associations. Woodcuts. 16mo. 1s.

———— SOUTHERN CATHEDRALS OF ENGLAND. Woodcuts. Post 8vo. (*Nearly Ready.*)

———— PARIS. Post 8vo. (*In preparation.*)

———— FAMILIAR QUOTATIONS. Chiefly from English Authors. *Third Edition.* Fcap. 8vo. 5s.

———— ARCHITECTURE. Being a Concise and Popular Account of the Different Styles prevailing in all Ages and Countries. By James Fergusson. *Fourth Thousand.* With 850 Illustrations. 8vo. 26s.

———— ARTS OF THE MIDDLE AGES AND RE-naissance. By M. Jules Labarte. With 200 Illustrations. 8vo. 18s.

HEAD'S (Sir Francis) Rough Notes of some Rapid Journeys across the Pampas and over the Andes. Post 8vo. 2s. 6d.

———— Descriptive Essays: contributed to the "Quarterly Review." 2 Vols. Post 8vo. 18s.

———— Bubbles from the Brunnen of Nassau. By an Old Man. *Sixth Edition.* 16mo. 5s.

———— Emigrant. *Sixth Edition.* Fcap. 8vo. 2s. 6d.

———— Stokers and Pokers; or, the London and North-Western Railway. Post 8vo. 2s. 6d.

———— Defenceless State of Great Britain. Post 8vo. 12s.

———— Faggot of French Sticks; or, Sketches of Paris. *New Edition.* 2 Vols. Post 8vo. 12s.

———— Fortnight in Ireland. *Second Edition.* Map. 8vo. 12s.

———— (Sir George) Forest Scenes and Incidents in Canada. *Second Edition.* Post 8vo. 10s.

———— Home Tour through the Manufacturing Districts of England, Scotland, and Ireland, including the Channel Islands, and the Isle of Man. *Third Edition.* 2 Vols. Post 8vo. 12s.

———— (Sir Edmund) Handbook of Painting—the Spanish and French Schools. With Illustrations. Post 8vo.

———— Shall and Will; or, Two Chapters on Future Auxiliary Verbs. *Second Edition, Enlarged.* Fcap. 8vo. 4s.

HEIRESS (The) in Her Minority; or, The Progress of Character. By the Author of "Bertha's Journal." 2 Vols. 12mo. 18s.

HERODOTUS. A New English Version. Edited with Notes, and Essays. By Rev G Rawlinson, assisted by Sir Henry Rawlinson, and Sir J. G. Wilkinson. Maps and Woodcuts. 4 Vols. 8vo. 18s. each.

HERVEY'S (Lord) Memoirs of the Reign of George the Second, from his Accession to the Death of Queen Caroline. Edited, with Notes by Mr. Croker. Second Edition. Portrait. 2 Vols. 8vo. 21s.

HICKMAN'S (Wm.) Treatise on the Law and Practice of Naval Courts Martial. 8vo. 10s. 6d.

HILLARD'S (G. S.) Six Months in Italy. 2 Vols. Post 8vo. 16s.

HISTORY OF ENGLAND AND FRANCE under the House of Lancaster. With an Introductory View of the Early Reformation. Second Edition. 8vo. 15s.

HOLLAND'S (Rev. W. B.) Psalms and Hymns, selected and adapted to the various Solemnities of the Church. Third Edition. 24mo. 1s. 3d.

HOLLWAY'S (J. G.) Month in Norway. Fcap. 8vo. 2s.

HONEY BEE (The). An Essay. By Rev. Thomas James. Reprinted from the "Quarterly Review." Fcap. 8vo. 1s.

HOOK'S (Dean) Church Dictionary. Eighth Edition. 8vo. 16s.

———— Discourses on the Religious Controversies of the Day. 8vo. 9s.

———— (Theodore) Life. By J. G. Lockhart. Reprinted from the "Quarterly Review." Fcap. 8vo. 1s.

HOOKER'S (Dr. J. D.) Himalayan Journals; or, Notes of an Oriental Naturalist in Bengal, the Sikkim and Nepal Himalayas, the Khasia Mountains, &c. Second Edition. Woodcuts. 2 vols. Post 8vo. 18s.

HOOPER'S (Lieut.) Ten Months among the Tents of the Tuski; with Incidents of an Arctic Boat Expedition in Search of Sir John Franklin. Plates, 8vo. 14s.

HORACE (Works of). Edited by Dean Milman. With 300 Woodcuts. Crown 8vo. 21s.

———— (Life of). By Dean Milman. Woodcuts, and coloured Borders. 8vo. 9s.

HOSPITALS AND SISTERHOODS. By a Lady. Fcap. 8vo. 3s. 6d.

HOUSTOUN'S (Mrs.) Yacht Voyage to Texas and the Gulf of Mexico. Plates. 2 Vols. Post 8vo. 21s.

c

HOME AND COLONIAL LIBRARY. Complete in 70 Parts.
Post 8vo, 2s. 6d. each, or bound in 34 Volumes, cloth.

CONTENTS OF THE SERIES.

THE BIBLE IN SPAIN. By George Borrow.
JOURNALS IN INDIA. By Bishop Heber.
TRAVELS IN THE HOLY LAND. By Captains Irby and Mangles.
THE SIEGE OF GIBRALTAR. By John Drinkwater.
MOROCCO AND THE MOORS. By J. Drummond Hay.
LETTERS FROM THE BALTIC. By a Lady.
THE AMBER-WITCH. By Lady Duff Gordon.
OLIVER CROMWELL & JOHN BUNYAN. By Robert Southey
NEW SOUTH WALES. By Mrs. Meredith.
LIFE OF SIR FRANCIS DRAKE. By John Barrow.
FATHER RIPA'S MEMOIRS OF THE COURT OF CHINA.
A RESIDENCE IN THE WEST INDIES. By M. G. Lewis.
SKETCHES OF PERSIA. By Sir John Malcolm.
THE FRENCH IN ALGIERS. By Lady Duff Gordon.
VOYAGE OF A NATURALIST. By Charles Darwin.
HISTORY OF THE FALL OF THE JESUITS.
LIFE OF LOUIS PRINCE OF CONDE. By Lord Mahon.
GIPSIES OF SPAIN. By George Borrow.
THE MARQUESAS. By Hermann Melville.
LIVONIAN TALES. By a Lady.
MISSIONARY LIFE IN CANADA. By Rev. J. Abbott.
SALE'S BRIGADE IN AFFGHANISTAN. By Rev. G. R. Gleig.
LETTERS FROM MADRAS. By a Lady.
HIGHLAND SPORTS. By Charles St. John.
JOURNEYS ACROSS THE PAMPAS. By Sir F. B. Head.
GATHERINGS FROM SPAIN. By Richard Ford.
SIEGES OF VIENNA BY THE TURKS. By Lord Ellesmere.
SKETCHES OF GERMAN LIFE. By Sir A. Gordon.
ADVENTURES IN THE SOUTH SEAS. By Hermann Melville.
STORY OF BATTLE OF WATERLOO. By Rev. G. R. Gleig
A VOYAGE UP THE RIVER AMAZON. By W. H. Edwards.
THE WAYSIDE CROSS. By Capt. Milman.
MANNERS & CUSTOMS OF INDIA. By Rev. C. Acland.
CAMPAIGNS AT WASHINGTON. By Rev. G. R. Gleig.
ADVENTURES IN MEXICO. By G. F. Ruxton.
PORTUGAL AND GALLICIA. By Lord Carnarvon.
LIFE OF LORD CLIVE. By Rev. G. R. Gleig.
BUSH LIFE IN AUSTRALIA. By H. W. Haygarth.
THE AUTOBIOGRAPHY OF HENRY STEFFENS.
SHORT LIVES OF THE POETS. By Thomas Campbell.
HISTORICAL ESSAYS. By Lord Mahon.
LONDON & NORTH-WESTERN RAILWAY. By Sir F. B. Head.
ADVENTURES IN THE LIBYAN DESERT. By Bayle St. John
A RESIDENCE AT SIERRA LEONE. By a Lady.
LIFE OF GENERAL MUNRO. By Rev. G. R. Gleig.
MEMOIRS OF SIR FOWELL BUXTON. By his Son.

HUME (The Student's). A History of England, from the Invasion of Julius Cæsar. Based on Hume's History, and continued to 1858. *Tenth Thousand.* Woodcuts. Post 8vo. 7s. 6d.

HUTCHINSON (Colonel) on Dog-Breaking; the most expeditious, certain, and easy Method, whether great Excellence or only Mediocrity be required. *Third Edition.* Woodcuts. Post 8vo. 9s.

HUTTON'S (H. E.) Principia Græca; an **Introduction** to the Study of Greek. Comprehending Grammar, Delectus, and Exercise-book, with Vocabularies. 12mo. 2s. **6d.**

IRBY AND MANGLES' Travels in Egypt, Nubia, Syria, **and** the Holy Land, including a Journey round the Dead Sea, and **through** the **Country** east of the Jordan. Post 8vo. 2s. 6d.

JAMES' (Rev. Thomas) Fables of Æsop. A New Translation, with Historical Preface. With 100 Woodcuts by Tenniel and Wolf. *Twenty-sixth Thousand.* Post 8vo. 2s. 6d.

JAMESON'S (Mrs.) Memoirs of the Early Italian Painters, and of the Progress of Italian Painting In Italy. *New Edition, revised and enlarged.* With very many Woodcuts. Post 8vo. 12s. (*Uniform with Kugler's Handbooks.*)

JAPAN AND THE JAPANESE. Described from the Accounts of Recent Dutch Travellers. *New Edition.* Post 8vo. 6s.

JARDINE'S (David) Narrative of the Gunpowder Plot. *New Edition.* Post 8vo. 7s. **6d.**

JERVIS'S (Capt.) Manual of Operations **in** the Field, for the Use of Officers. Post 8vo. 9s. 6d.

JESSE'S (Edward) Favorite Haunts and Rural Studies; or Visits to Spots of Interest in the Vicinity of Windsor and Eton. Woodcuts. Post 8vo. 12s.

———— Scenes and Occupations of Country Life. With Recollections of Natural History. *Third Edition.* Woodcuts. Fcap. 8vo. 6s.

———— Gleanings in Natural History. With Anecdotes of the Sagacity and Instinct of Animals. *Eighth Edition.* Fcap. 8vo. 6s.

JOHNSON'S (Dr. Samuel) Life: By James Boswell. Including the Tour to the Hebrides. Edited by the late Mr. Croker. *Third Edition.* Portraits. Royal 8vo. 10s. sewed; 12s. cloth.

———— Lives of the most eminent English Poets. **Edited** by Peter Cunningham. 3 vols. 8vo. 22s. 6d. (Murray's British Classics.)

JOHNSTON'S (Wm.) England: Social, **Political,** and Industrial, in 19th Century. 2 Vols. Post 8vo. 18s.

JOURNAL OF A NATURALIST. *Fourth Edition.* Woodcuts. Post 8vo. 9s. 6d.

JOWETT'S (Rev. B.) Commentary on St. Paul's Epistles to the Thessalonians, Galatians, **and Romans.** *Second Edition.* 2 Vols. 8vo. 30s.

JONES' (Rev. R.) Literary Remains. With a Prefatory Notice. By Rev. **W.** Whewell, D.D. Portrait. 8vo. 14s.

KEN'S (Bishop) Life. By A Layman. *Second Edition.* Portrait. 2 Vols. 8vo. 18s.

———— (Bishop) Exposition of the Apostles' Creed. Extracted from his "Practice of Divine **Love.**" *New Edition.* Fcap. 1s. 6d.

———— Approach to the Holy Altar. Extracted from his "Manual of Prayer" and "Practice of Divine Love." *New Edition.* Fcap. 8vo. 1s. 6d.

c 2

KING'S (Rev. S. W.) Italian Valleys of the Alps; a Tour through all the Romantic and less-frequented "Vals" of Northern Piedmont, from the Tarentaise to the Gries. With Illustrations. Crown 8vo. 18s.

KING EDWARD VIth's Latin Grammar; or, an Introduction to the Latin Tongue, for the Use of Schools. 12th Edition. 12mo. 3s. 6d.

―――――――――― First Latin Book; or, the Accidence, Syntax and Prosody, with an English Translation for the Use of Junior Classes. Third Edition. 12mo. 2s.

KINGLAKE'S (A. W.) History of the War in the Crimea. Based chiefly upon the Private Papers of Field Marshal Lord Raglan, and other authentic materials. Vols. I. and II. 8vo.

KNAPP'S (J. A.) English Roots and Ramifications; or, the Derivation and Meaning of Divers Words. Fcap. 8vo. 4s.

KUGLER'S (Dr. Franz) Handbook to the History of Painting (the Italian Schools). Translated from the German. Edited, with Notes, by Sir Charles Eastlake. Third Edition. Woodcuts. 2 Vols. Post 8vo. 30s.

―――――――――― (the German, Dutch, and Flemish Schools). Translated from the German. A New Edition. Edited, with Notes. By Dr. Waagen. Woodcuts. Post 8vo. Nearly Ready.

LABARTE'S (M. Jules) Handbook of the Arts of the Middle Ages and Renaissance. With 200 Woodcuts. 8vo. 18s.

LABORDE'S (Leon de) Journey through Arabia Petraea, to Mount Sinai, and the Excavated City of Petraea,—the Edom of the Prophecies. Second Edition. With Plates. 8vo. 18s.

LANE'S (E. W.) Arabian Nights. Translated from the Arabic, with Explanatory Notes. A New Edition. Edited by E. Stanley Poole. With 600 Woodcuts. 3 Vols. 8vo. 42s.

―――――――――― Manners and Customs of the Modern Egyptians. A New Edition, with Additions and Improvements by the Author. Edited by E. Stanley Poole. Woodcuts. 8vo. 18s.

LATIN GRAMMAR (King Edward the VIth's.) For the Use of Schools. Twelfth Edition. 12mo. 3s. 6d.

―――――――――― First Book (King Edward VI.); or, the Accidence, Syntax, and Prosody, with English Translation for Junior Classes. Third Edition. 12mo. 2s.

LAYARD'S (A. H.) Nineveh and its Remains. Being a Narrative of Researches and Discoveries amidst the Ruins of Assyria. With an Account of the Chaldean Christians of Kurdistan; the Yezedis, or Devil-worshippers; and an Enquiry into the Manners and Arts of the Ancient Assyrians. Sixth Edition. Plates and Woodcuts. 2 Vols. 8vo. 36s.

―――――――――― Nineveh and Babylon; being the Result of a Second Expedition to Assyria. Fourteenth Thousand. Plates. 8vo. 21s. Or Fine Paper, 2 Vols. 8vo. 30s.

―――――――――― Popular Account of Nineveh. 15th Edition. With Woodcuts. Post 8vo. 5s.

LESLIE'S (C. R.) Handbook for Young Painters. With Illustrations. Post 8vo. 10s. 6d.

―――――――――― Life of Sir Joshua Reynolds. With an Account of his Works, and a Sketch of his Cotemporaries. Fcap. 4to. In the Press.

LEAKE'S (Col. W. Martin) Topography of Athens, with Remarks
on its Antiquities; to which is added, the Demi of Attica. *Second
Edition.* Plates. 2 Vols. 8vo. 30s.

———— Travels in Northern Greece. Maps. 4 Vols. 8vo. 60s.

———— Disputed Questions of Ancient Geography. Map.
8vo. 6s. 6d.

———— Numismata Hellenica. A Catalogue of Greek Coins.
With Map and Appendix. 4to. 63s.

————— A Supplement to Numismata Hellenica; Completing a
descriptive Catalogue of Twelve Thousand Greek Coins, with Notes
Geographical and Historical. 4to.

———— Peloponnesiaca : A Supplement to Travels in the Morea.
8vo. 15s.

———— Thoughts on the Degradation of Science in England.
8vo. 3s. 6d.

LETTERS FROM THE SHORES OF THE BALTIC. By a
Lady. Post 8vo. 2s. 6d.

————————— Madras ; or, First Impressions of Life and
Manners in India. By a Lady. Post 8vo. 2s. 6d.

————————— Sierra Leone, written to Friends at Home.
By a Lady. Edited by Mrs. Norton. Post 8vo. 6s.

————————— Head Quarters; or, The Realities of the War
in the Crimea. By a Staff Officer. *Popular Edition.* Plans.
Post 8vo. 6s.

LEXINGTON (The) PAPERS; or, Some Account of the Courts
of London and Vienna at the end of the 17th Century. Edited by Hon.
H. Manners Sutton. 8vo. 14s.

LEWIS' (Sir G. C.) Essay on the Government of Dependencies.
8vo. 12s.

———— Glossary of Provincial Words used in Herefordshire and
some of the adjoining Counties. 12mo. 4s. 6d.

———— (Lady Theresa) Friends and Contemporaries of the
Lord Chancellor Clarendon, illustrative of Portraits in his Gallery.
With a Descriptive Account of the Pictures, and Origin of the Collec-
tion. Portraits. 3 Vols. 8vo. 42s.

———— (M. G.) Journal of a Residence among the Negroes in the
West Indies. Post 8vo. 2s. 6d.

LIDDELL'S (Dean) History of Rome. From the Earliest Times
to the Establishment of the Empire. With the History of Literature
and Art. *Library Edition.* 2 Vols. 8vo. 28s.

———— STUDENT'S HISTORY OF ROME. Abridged from
the Larger Work. *Fifteenth Thousand.* With 100 Woodcuts. Post
8vo. 7s. 6d.

LINDSAY'S (Lord) Lives of the Lindsays ; or, a Memoir of the
Houses of Crawford and Balcarres. With Extracts from Official Papers
and Personal Narratives. *Second Edition.* 3 Vols. 8vo. 24s.

———— Report of the Claim of James, Earl of Crawford and
Balcarres, to the Original Dukedom of Montrose, created in 1488.
Folio. 15s.

LITTLE ARTHUR'S HISTORY OF ENGLAND. By Lady
Callcott. *Nineteenth Edition.* With 20 Woodcuts. Fcap. 8vo.
2s. 6d.

LIVINGSTONE'S (Rev. Dr.) Missionary Travels and Researches
in South Africa; including a Sketch of Sixteen Years' Residence in
the Interior of Africa, and a Journey from the Cape of Good Hope to
Loanda on the West Coast; thence across the Continent, down the
River Zambesi, to the Eastern Ocean. *Thirtieth Thousand*. Map,
Plates, and Index. 8vo. 21*s.*

LIVONIAN TALES.—The Disponent.—The Wolves.—The Jewess.
By the Author of "Letters from the Baltic." Post 8vo. 2*s.* 6*d.*

LOCKHART'S (J. G.) Ancient Spanish Ballads. **Historical and**
Romantic. Translated, with Notes. *Illustrated Edition*. 4to. 21*s.* Or,
Popular Edition. Post 8vo. 2*s.* 6*d.*

————————— Life of Robert Burns. *Fifth Edition*. Fcap. 8vo. **3***s.*

LOUDON'S (Mrs.) Instructions in Gardening for Ladies. With
Directions and Calendar of Operations for Every Month. *Eighth
Edition*. Woodcuts. Fcap. 8vo. 5*s.*

————————— Modern Botany; a Popular Introduction to the
Natural System of Plants. *Second Edition*. Woodcuts. Fcap. 8vo. 6*s.*

LOWE'S (Sir Hudson) Letters and Journals, during the Captivity
of Napoleon at St. Helena. By William Forsyth. Portrait. 3 Vols.
8vo. **45***s.*

LUCKNOW : A Lady's Diary of the Siege. Written for Friends
at Home. *Fourth Thousand*. Fcap. 8vo. 4*s.* 6*d.*

LYELL'S (Sir Charles) Principles of Geology; **or,** the Modern
Changes of the Earth and its Inhabitants considered as illustrative of
Geology. *Ninth Edition*. Woodcuts. 8vo. 18*s.*

————————— Visits to the United States, 1841-46. *Second Edition*.
Plates. 4 Vols. Post 8vo. 24*s.*

MAHON'S (Lord) History of England, **from the** Peace of Utrecht
to the Peace of Versailles, 1713—83. *Library Edition*. 7 Vols. 8vo. 93*s.*
Popular Edition. 7 Vols. Post 8vo. 35*s.*

————————— "Forty-Five;" a Narrative of the Rebellion in Scotland. Post 8vo. 3*s.*

————————— History of British India from its Origin till the Peace
of 1783. Post 8vo. 3*s.* 6*d.* .

————————— History of **the War of** the Succession in Spain. *Second
Edition*. Map. 8vo. **15***s.*

————————— Spain under Charles **the Second**; **or,** Extracts from the
Correspondence of the Hon. Alexander Stanhope, British Minister at
Madrid from 1690 to 1700. *Second Edition*. Post 8vo. 6*s.* 6*d.*

————————— Life of Louis Prince of Condé, surnamed the Great.
Post 8vo. 6*s.*

————————— Life of Belisarius. *Second Edition*. Post 8vo. 10*s.* 6*d.*

————————— Historical and Critical Essays. Post 8vo. 6*s.*

————————— Story of Joan of Arc. Fcap. 8vo. 1*s.*

————————— Addresses Delivered at Manchester, Leeds, and Birmingham. Fcap. 8vo. 1*s.*

McCLINTOCK'S (Capt.) Narrative of **the** Discovery of the Fate
of Sir John Franklin and his Companions, in the Arctic Seas. With
Preface, by Sir Roderick Murchison. Map and Illustrations. 8vo. 16*s.*

McCOSH (Rev. Dr.) On the intuitive Convictions of the Mind. 8vo.

M'CULLOCH'S (J. R.) Collected Edition of RICARDO's Political Works. With Notes and Memoir. *Second Edition.* 8vo. 16s.

MALCOLM'S (SIR JOHN) Sketches of Persia. *Third Edition.* Post 8vo. 6s.

MANSEL'S (REV. H. L.) Bampton Lectures. The Limits of Religious Thought Examined. *Fourth and cheaper Edition.* Post 8vo. 7s. 6d.

——————— Examination of Professor Maurice's Strictures on the Bampton Lectures of 1858. *Second Edition.* 8vo. 2s. 6d.

MANTELL'S (GIDEON A.) Thoughts on Animalcules; or, the Invisible World, as revealed by the Microscope. *Second Edition.* Plates. 16mo. 6s.

MANUAL OF SCIENTIFIC ENQUIRY, Prepared for the Use of Officers and Travellers. By various Writers. *Third Edition revised* by the Rev. R. MAIN. Maps. Post 8vo. 9s. (*Published by order of the Lords of the Admiralty.*)

MARKHAM'S (MRS.) History of England. From the First Invasion by the Romans, down to the fourteenth year of Queen Victoria's Reign. 118th *Edition.* Woodcuts. 12mo. 6s.

——————— History of France. From the Conquest by the Gauls, to the Death of Louis Philippe. *Sixtieth Edition.* Woodcuts. 12mo. 6s.

——————— History of Germany. From the Invasion by Marius, to the present time. *Fifteenth Edition.* Woodcuts. 12mo. 6s.

——————— History of Greece. From the Earliest Times to the Roman Conquest. With the History of Literature and Art. By Dr. WM. SMITH. *Twentieth Thousand.* Woodcuts. 12mo. 7s. 6d. (*Questions.* 12mo. 2s.)

——————— History of Rome, from the Earliest Times to the Establishment of the Empire. With the History of Literature and Art. By DEAN LIDDELL. *Fifteenth Thousand.* Woodcuts. 12mo. 7s. 6d.

MARKLAND'S (J. H.) Reverence due to Holy Places. *Third Edition.* Fcap. 8vo. 2s.

MARRYAT'S (JOSEPH) History of Modern and Mediæval Pottery and Porcelain. With a Description of the Manufacture, a Glossary, and a List of Monograms. *Second Edition.* Plates and Woodcuts. 8vo. 31s. 6d.

MATTHIÆ'S (AUGUSTUS) Greek Grammar for Schools. Abridged from the Larger Grammar. By Blomfield. *Ninth Edition.* Revised by EDWARDS. 12mo. 3s.

MAUREL'S (JULES) Essay on the Character, Actions, and Writings of the Duke of Wellington. *Second Edition.* Fcap. 8vo. 1s. 6d.

MAWE'S (H. L.) Journal of a Passage from the Pacific to the Atlantic, crossing the Andes in the Northern Provinces of Peru, and descending the great River Maranon. 8vo. 12s.

MAXIMS AND HINTS for an Angler, and the Miseries of Fishing. By RICHARD PENN. *New Edition.* Woodcuts. 12mo. 1s.

MAYO'S (DR.) Pathology of the Human Mind. Fcap. 8vo. 5s. 6d.

MELVILLE'S (HERMANN) Typee and Omoo; or, Adventures amongst the Marquesas and South Sea Islands. 2 Vols. Post 8vo.

MENDELSSOHN'S (FELIX BARTHOLDY) Life. By JULES BENEDICT. 8vo. 2s. 6d.

MEREDITH'S (Mrs. Charles) Notes and Sketches of New South
Wales, during a Residence from 1839 to 1844. Post 8vo. 2s. 6d.

———————— Tasmania, during a Residence of Nine Years.
With Illustrations. 2 Vols. Post 8vo. 18s.

MERRIFIELD (Mrs.) on the Arts of Painting in Oil, Miniature,
Mosaic, and Glass; Gilding, Dyeing, and the Preparation of Colours
and Artificial Gems, described in several old Manuscripts. 2 Vols. 8vo.
30s.

MILLS (Arthur) India in 1858; A Summary of the Existing
Administration—Political, Fiscal, and Judicial; with Laws and Public
Documents, from the earliest to the present time. Second Edition. With
Coloured Revenue Map. 8vo. 10s. 6d.

MITCHELL'S (Thomas) Plays of Aristophanes. With English
Notes. 8vo.—1. CLOUDS, 10s.—2. WASPS, 10s.—3. FROGS, 15s.

MILMAN'S (Dean) History of Christianity, from the Birth of
Christ to the Extinction of Paganism in the Roman Empire. 3 Vols.
8vo. 36s.

———————— History of Latin Christianity; including that of the
Popes to the Pontificate of Nicholas V. Second Edition. 6 Vols. 8vo. 72s.

———————— Character and Conduct of the Apostles considered as
an Evidence of Christianity. 8vo. 10s. 6d.

———————— Life and Works of Horace. With 300 Woodcuts.
New Edition. 2 Vols. Crown 8vo. 30s.

———————— Poetical Works. Plates. 3 Vols. Fcap. 8vo. 18s.

———————— Fall of Jerusalem. Fcap. 8vo. 1s.

———————— (Capt. E. A.) Wayside Cross; or, the Raid of Gomez.
A Tale of the Carlist War. Post 8vo. 2s. 6d.

MODERN DOMESTIC COOKERY. Founded on Principles of
Economy and Practical Knowledge, and adapted for Private Families.
New Edition. Woodcuts. Fcap. 8vo. 5s.

MOLTKE'S (Baron) Russian Campaigns on the Danube and the
Passage of the Balkan, 1828—9. Plans. 8vo. 14s.

MONASTERY AND THE MOUNTAIN CHURCH. By Author
of "Sunlight through the Mist." Woodcuts. 16mo. 4s.

MOORE'S (Thomas) Life and Letters of Lord Byron. 6 Vols.
Fcap. 8vo. 18s.

———————— Life and Letters of Lord Byron. With Portraits.
Royal 8vo. 9s. sewed, or 10s. 6d. in cloth.

MOZLEY'S (Rev. J. B.) Treatise on the Augustinian Doctrine of
Predestination. 8vo. 14s.

———————— Primitive Doctrine of Baptismal Regeneration. 8vo. 7s. 6d.

MUCK MANUAL (The) for the Use of Farmers. A Practical Treatise
on the Chemical Properties, Management, and Application of Manures.
By Frederick Falkner. Second Edition. Fcap. 8vo. 5s.

MUNDY'S (Gen.) Pen and Pencil Sketches during a Tour
in India. Third Edition. Plates. Post 8vo. 7s. 6d.

MUNRO'S (General Sir Thomas) Life and Letters. By the Rev.
G. R. Gleig. Post 8vo. 6s.

MURCHISON'S (Sir Roderick) Russia in Europe and the Ural
Mountains; Geologically Illustrated. With Coloured Maps, Plates,
Sections, &c. 2 Vols. Royal 4to.

———————— Siluria ; or, a History of the Oldest Rocks containing Organic Remains. *Third Edition*. Map and Plates. 8vo. 42s.

MURRAY'S (Capt. A.) Naval Life and Services of Admiral Sir
Philip Durham. 8vo. 5s. 6d.

MURRAY'S RAILWAY READING. For all classes of Readers.

[The following are published:]

WELLINGTON. By Lord Ellesmere. 6d.
NIMROD ON THE CHASE, 1s.
ESSAYS FROM "THE TIMES." 2 Vols. 8s.
MUSIC AND DRESS. 1s.
LAYARD'S ACCOUNT OF NINEVEH. 5s.
MILMAN'S FALL OF JERUSALEM. 1s.
MAHON'S "FORTY-FIVE." 3s.
LIFE OF THEODORE HOOK. 1s.
DEEDS OF NAVAL DARING, 2 Vols. 5s.
THE HONEY BEE. 1s.
JAMES' ÆSOP'S FABLES. 2s. 6d.
NIMROD ON THE TURF. 1s. 6d.
OLIPHANT'S NEPAUL. 2s. 6d.
ART OF DINING. 1s. 6d.
HALLAM'S LITERARY ESSAYS. 2s.

MAHON'S JOAN OF ARC. 1s.
HEAD'S EMIGRANT. 2s. 6d.
NIMROD ON THE ROAD, 1s.
WILKINSON'S ANCIENT EGYPTIANS. 12s.
CROKER ON THE GUILLOTINE. 1s.
HOLLWAY'S NORWAY. 2s.
MAUREL'S WELLINGTON. 1s. 6d.
CAMPBELL'S LIFE OF BACON. 2s. 6d.
THE FLOWER GARDEN. 1s.
LOCKHART'S SPANISH BALLADS. 2s. 6d.
LUCAS ON HISTORY. 6d.
BEAUTIES OF BYRON. 3s.
TAYLOR'S NOTES FROM LIFE. 2s.
REJECTED ADDRESSES. 1s.
PENN'S HINTS ON ANGLING. 1s.

MUSIC AND DRESS. Two Essays, by a Lady. Reprinted from
the "Quarterly Review." Fcap. 8vo. 1s.

NAPIER'S (Sir Wm.) English Battles and Sieges of the Peninsular
War. *Third Edition*. Portrait. Post 8vo. 10s. 6d.

———————— Life and Opinions of General Sir Charles Napier;
chiefly derived from his Journals, Letters, and Familiar Correspondence. *Second Edition*. Portraits. 4 Vols. Post 8vo. 48s.

NAUTICAL ALMANACK (The). Royal 8vo. 2s. 6d. (*Published
by Authority*.)

NAVY LIST (The Quarterly). (*Published by Authority*.)
Post 8vo. 2s. 6d.

NELSON (The Pious Robert), his Life and Times. By Rev. C. T.
Secretan, M.A. Portrait. 8vo. 12s.

NEWBOLD'S (Lieut.) Straits of Malacca, Penang, and Singapore.
2 Vols. 8vo. 26s.

NEWDEGATE'S (C. N.) Customs' Tariffs of all Nations; collected
and arranged up to the year 1855. 4to. 30s.

NICHOLLS' (Sir George) History of the British Poor : Being
an Historical Account of the English, Scotch, and Irish Poor Law : in
connection with the Condition of the People. 4 Vols. 8vo.

The work may be had separately :—
English Poor-Laws. 2 Vols. 8vo. 28s.
Irish Poor. 8vo. 14s.—Scotch Poor. 8vo. 12s.

———————— (Rev. H. G.) Historical and Descriptive Account
of the Forest of Dean, derived from Personal Observation and
other Sources, Public, Private, Legendary, and Local. Woodcuts, &c.
Post 8vo. 10s. 6d.

NICOLAS' (Sir Harris) Historic Peerage of England. Exhi-
biting, under Alphabetical Arrangement, the Origin, Descent, and
Present State of every Title of Peerage which has existed in this
Country since the Conquest. Being a New Edition of the "Synopsis of
the Peerage." Revised, Corrected, and Continued to the Present Time.
By William Courthope, Somerset Herald. 8vo. 30s.

NIMROD On the Chace—The Turf—and The Road. Reprinted from the "Quarterly Review." Woodcuts. Fcap. 8vo. 3s. 6d.

O'CONNOR'S (R.) Field Sports of France; or, Hunting, Shooting, and Fishing on the Continent. Woodcuts. 8vo. 7s. 6d.

OLIPHANT'S (LAURENCE) Journey to Katmandu, with Visit to the Camp of the Nepaulese Ambassador. Fcap. 8vo. 2s. 6d.

OWEN'S (PROFESSOR) Manual of Fossil Mammals. Including the substance of the course of Lectures on Osteology and Palæontology of the class Mammalia, delivered at the Metropolitan School of Science, Jermyn Street. Illustrations. 8vo. [In the Press.

OXENHAM'S (REV. W.) English Notes for Latin Elegiacs; designed for early Proficients in the Art of Latin Versification, with Prefatory Rules of Composition in Elegiac Metre. Third Edition. 12mo. 4s.

PAGET'S (JOHN) Hungary and Transylvania. With Remarks on their Condition, Social, Political, and Economical. Third Edition. Woodcuts. 2 Vols. 8vo. 18s.

PARIS' (Dr.) Philosophy in Sport made Science in Earnest; or, the First Principles of Natural Philosophy inculcated by aid of the Toys and Sports of Youth. Eighth Edition. Woodcuts. Post 8vo. 9s.

PARKYNS' (MANSFIELD) Personal Narrative of Three Years' Residence and Adventures in Abyssinia. Woodcuts. 2 Vols. 8vo. 30s.

PEEL'S (SIR ROBERT) Memoirs. Left in MSS. Edited by EARL STANHOPE and the Right Hon. EDWARD CARDWELL. 2 Vols. Post 8vo. 7s. 6d. each.

PEILE'S (REV. DR.) Agamemnon and Choephoræ of Æschylus. A New Edition of the Text, with Notes. Second Edition. 2 Vols. 8vo. 9s. each.

PENN'S (RICHARD) Maxims and Hints for an Angler, and the Miseries of Fishing. To which is added, Maxims and Hints for a Chess-player. New Edition. Woodcuts. Fcap. 8vo. 1s.

PENROSE'S (REV. JOHN) Faith and Practice; an Exposition of the Principles and Duties of Natural and Revealed Religion. Post 8vo. 8s. 6d.

—————— (F. C.) Principles of Athenian Architecture, and the Optical Refinements exhibited in the Construction of the Ancient Buildings at Athens, from a Survey. With 40 Plates. Folio. 5l. 5s. (Published under the direction of the Dilettanti Society.)

PERCY'S (JOHN, M.D.) Metallurgy; or, the Art of Extracting Metals from their Ores and adapting them to various purposes of Manufacture. Illustrations. 8vo. [In the Press.

PERRY'S (SIR ERSKINE) Bird's-Eye View of India. With Extracts from a Journal kept in the Provinces, Nepaul, &c. Fcap. 8vo. 5s.

PHILLIPS' (JOHN) Memoirs of William Smith, LL.D. (the Geologist). Portrait. 8vo. 7s. 6d.

—————— Geology of Yorkshire, The Yorkshire Coast, and the Mountain-Limestone District. Plates 4to. Part I., 20s.—Part II., 30s.

—————— Rivers, Mountains, and Sea Coast of Yorkshire. With Essays on the Climate, Scenery, and Ancient Inhabitants of the Country. Second Edition, with 36 Plates. 8vo. 15s.

PHILPOTT'S (BISHOP) Letters to the late Charles Butler, on the Theological parts of his "Book of the Roman Catholic Church;" with Remarks on certain Works of Dr. Milner and Dr. Lingard, and on some parts of the Evidence of Dr. Doyle. Second Edition. 8vo. 16s.

PHIPPS' (HON. EDMUND) Memoir, Correspondence, Literary and Unpublished Diaries of Robert Plumer Ward. Portrait. 2 Vols. 8vo. 28s.

POPE'S (ALEXANDER) Works. An entirely New Edition. Edited, with Notes. 8vo. [In the Press.

PORTER'S (Rev. J. L.) Five Years in Damascus. With Travels to Palmyra, Lebanon, and other Scripture Sites. Map and Woodcuts. 2 vols. Post 8vo. 21s.

———— Handbook for Syria and Palestine : including an Account of the Geography, History, Antiquities, and Inhabitants of these Countries, the Peninsula of Sinai, Edom, and the Syrian Desert. Maps. 2 Vols. Post 8vo. 24s.

———— (Mrs.) Rational Arithmetic for Schools and for Private Instruction. 12mo. 3s. 6d.

PRAYER-BOOK (The Illustrated), with 1000 Illustrations of Borders, Initials, Vignettes, &c. Medium 8vo. Cloth, 21s.; Calf, 31s. 6d.; Morocco, 42s.

PRECEPTS FOR THE CONDUCT OF LIFE. Exhortations to a Virtuous Course and Dissuasions from a Vicious Career. Extracted from the Scriptures. Second Edition. Fcap. 8vo. 1s.

PRINSEP'S (Jas.) Essays on Indian Antiquities, Historic, Numismatic, and Palæographic, with Tables, illustrative of Indian History, Chronology, Modern Coinages, Weights, Measures, &c. Edited by Edward Thomas. Illustrations. 2 Vols. 8vo. 52s. 6d.

PROGRESS OF RUSSIA IN THE EAST. An Historical Summary, continued to the Present Time. With Map by Arrowsmith. Third Edition. 8vo. 6s. 6d.

PUSS IN BOOTS. With 12 Illustrations ; for Old and Young. By Otto Speckter. A New Edition. 16mo. 1s. 6d.

QUARTERLY REVIEW (The). 8vo. 6s.

RANKE'S (Leopold) Political and Ecclesiastical History of the Popes of Rome, during the Sixteenth and Seventeenth Centuries. Translated from the German by Mrs. Austin. Third Edition. 2 Vols. 8vo. 24s.

RAWLINSON'S (Rev. George) Herodotus. A New English Version. Edited with Notes and Essays. Assisted by Sir Henry Rawlinson and Sir J. G. Wilkinson. Maps and Woodcuts. 4 Vols. 8vo. 18s. each.

———— Historical Evidences of the truth of the Scripture Records stated anew, with special reference to the Doubts and Discoveries of Modern Times ; being the Bampton Lectures for 1859. 8vo. 14s.

REJECTED ADDRESSES (The). By James and Horace Smith. With Biographies of the Authors, and additional Notes. New Edition, with the Author's latest Corrections. Fcap. 8vo. 1s., or Fine Paper, with Portrait. Fcap. 8vo. 5s.

RENNIE'S (James) Insect Architecture. To which are added Chapters on the Ravages, the Preservation, for Purposes of Study, and the Classification of Insects. New Edition. Woodcuts. Post 8vo. 5s.

RICARDO'S (David) Political Works. With a Notice of his Life and Writings. By J. R. M'Culloch. New Edition. 8vo. 16s.

RIPA'S (Father) Memoirs during Thirteen Years' Residence at the Court of Peking, in the Service of the Emperor of China. Translated from the Italian. By Fortunato Prandi. Post 8vo. 2s. 6d.

ROBERTSON'S (Rev. J. C.) History of the Christian Church, From the Apostolic Age to the Pontificate of Gregory the Great, A.D. 590. Second and Revised Edition. Vol. 1. 8vo. 16s.

———— Second Period, from A.D. 590 to the Concordat of Worms. A.D. 1123. Vol. 2. 8vo. 18s.

———— Becket, Archbishop of Canterbury ; a Biography. Illustrations. Post 8vo. 9s.

ROBINSON'S (Rev. Dr.) Biblical Researches in the Holy Land. Being a Journal of Travels in 1838, and of Later Researches in 1852. With New Maps. 3 Vols. 8vo. 36s.
  ∗ The "Later Researches" may be had separately. 8vo. 15s.

ROMILLY'S (Sir Samuel) Memoirs and Political Diary. By his Sons. *Third Edition.* Portrait. 2 Vols. Fcap. 8vo. 12s.

ROSS'S (Sir James) Voyage of Discovery and Research in the Southern and Antarctic Regions during the years 1839-43. **Plates.** 2 Vols. 8vo. **36s.**

ROWLAND'S (David) Manual of the English Constitution; a Review of its Rise, Growth, and Present State. Post 8vo. 10s. 6d.

RUNDELL'S (Mrs.) Domestic Cookery, founded on Principles of Economy and Practice, and adapted for Private Families. *New and Revised Edition.* Woodcuts. Fcap. 8vo. 5s.

RUSSIA; A Memoir of the Remarkable Events which attended the Accession of the Emperor Nicholas. By Baron M. Korff, Secretary of State. 8vo. 10s. 6d. *(Published by Imperial Command.)*

RUXTON'S (George F.) Travels in Mexico; with Adventures among the Wild Tribes and Animals of the Prairies and Rocky Mountains. Post 8vo. 6s.

SALE'S (Lady) Journal of the Disasters in Affghanistan. *Eighth Edition.* Post 8vo. 12s.

—— (Sir Robert) Brigade in Affghanistan. With an Account of the Seizure and Defence of Jellalabad. By Rev. G. R. Gleig. Post 8vo. 2s. 6d.

SANDWITH'S (Humphry) Narrative of the Siege of Kars and of the Six Months' Resistance by the Turkish Garrison under General Williams. *Seventh Thousand.* Post 8vo. 3s. 6d.

SCOTT'S (G. Gilbert) Remarks on Secular and Domestic Architecture, Present and Future. *Second Edition.* 8vo. 9s.

SCROPE'S (William) Days of Deer-Stalking in the Forest of Atholl; with some Account of the Nature and Habits of the Red Deer. *Third Edition.* Woodcuts. Crown 8vo. 20s.

—— Days and Nights of Salmon Fishing in the Tweed; with a short Account of the Natural History and Habits of the Salmon. *Second Edition.* Woodcuts. Royal 8vo. 31s. 6d.

—— (G. P.) Memoir of Lord Sydenham, and his Administration in Canada. *Second Edition.* Portrait. 8vo. 9s. 6d.

—— Geology and Extinct Volcanos of Central France. *Second Edition,* revised and enlarged. Illustrations. Medium 8vo. 30s.

SHAFTESBURY (Lord Chancellor), Memoirs of his Early Life. With his Letters, Speeches, and other Papers. By W. D. Christie. Portrait. 8vo. 10s. 6d.

SHAW'S (Thos. B.) Outlines of English Literature, for the Use of Young Students. Post 8vo. 12s.

SIERRA LEONE; Described in a Series of Letters to Friends at Home. By A Lady. Edited by Mrs. Norton. Post 8vo. 6s.

SMILES' (Samuel) Life of George Stephenson. *Fifth Edition.* Portrait. 8vo. 16s.

—— Story of the Life of Stephenson. With Woodcuts. *Fifth Thousand.* Post 8vo. 6s.

—— Self Help. With Illustrations of Character and Conduct. Post 8vo. 6s.

SOMERVILLE'S (Mary) Physical Geography. *Fourth Edition.* Portrait. Post 8vo. 9s.

—— Connexion of the Physical Sciences. *Ninth Edition.* Woodcuts. Post 8vo. 9s.

SOUTH'S (John F.) Household Surgery; or, Hints on Emergencies. *Seventeenth Thousand.* Woodcuts. Fcp. 8vo. 4s. 6d.

SOUTHEY'S (Robert) Book of the Church; with Notes containing the Authorities, and an Index. *Seventh Edition.* Post 8vo. 7s. 6d.

—— Lives of John Bunyan & Oliver Cromwell. Post 8vo. 2s. 6d.

SMITH'S (WM., LL.D.) Dictionary of Greek and Roman Antiquities. *Second Edition.* With 500 Woodcuts. 8vo. 42s.
———— Smaller Dictionary of Greek and Roman Antiquities. Abridged from the above work. *Fourth Edition.* With 200 Woodcuts. Crown 8vo. 7s. 6d.
———— Dictionary of Greek and Roman Biography and Mythology. With 500 Woodcuts. 3 Vols. 8vo. 5l. 15s. 6d.
———— Dictionary of Greek and Roman Geography. **With** Woodcuts. 2 Vols. 8vo. 80s.
———— Atlas of Ancient Geography. 4to. [*In preparation.*
———— Classical Dictionary for the Higher Forms in Schools. Compiled from the above two works. *Fifth Edition.* With 750 Woodcuts. 8vo. 18s.
———— **Smaller** Classical Dictionary. Abridged **from the** above work. *Fifth Edition.* With 200 Woodcuts. **Crown 8vo. 7s. 6d.**
———— Latin - English Dictionary. Based upon **the Works** of Forcellini and Freund. *Seventh Thousand.* 8vo. 21s.
———— Smaller Latin-English Dictionary. Abridged **from the** above work. *Sixteenth Thousand.* Square 12mo. 7s 6d.
———— English-Latin Dictionary. 8vo. & 12mo. [*In preparation.*
———— Mediæval Latin-English Dictionary. Selected from the great work of DUCANGE. 8vo. [*In preparation.*
———— Dictionary of the Bible, **including** its Antiquities, Biography, Geography, **and Natural** History. **Woodcuts.** Vol. 1. 8vo. 42s. [*Nearly ready.*
———— Gibbon's History of **the** Decline and Fall of **the** Roman Empire. Edited, with Notes. **Portrait** and Map. 8 Vols. 8vo. 60s. (Murray's British Classics.)
———— Student's Gibbon; being the History **of** the Decline and Fall, Abridged. Incorporating the Researches of Recent Commentators. *Sixth Thousand.* Woodcuts. Post 8vo. 7s. 6d.
———— Student's History of Greece ; from the Earliest Times to the Roman Conquest. With the History of Literature and Art. *Twentieth Thousand.* Woodcuts. Crown 8vo. 7s. 6d. (Questions. 12mo. 2s.)
———— Smaller History of Greece for Junior Classes. Woodcuts. 12mo. 3s. 6d.
———— Student's **Hume.** A History of England from **the** Invasion of Julius Cæsar. Based on Hume's History, and continued to 1858. *Tenth Thousand.* Woodcuts. Post **8vo. 7s. 6d.**
———— Student's History of Rome ; from the **Earliest** Times to the Establishment of the Empire. With the **History** of Literature and Art. By H. G. LIDDELL, D.D. *Fifteenth* **Thousand.** Woodcuts. Crown 8vo. **7s. 6d.**
———— Principia Latina ; a **First Latin Course, comprehending** Grammar, Delectus, and Exercise Book, with **Vocabularies,** for the lower forms in Public and **Private Schools.** 12mo. 3s. 6d.
———— Principia Græca; an Introduction to **the** Study of Greek. Comprehending Grammar, Delectus, and Exercise-book with Vocabularies. For the Lower Forms. By H. E. HUTTON, M.A. 12mo. 2s. 6d.
———— (WM. JAS.) Grenville **Letters** and Diaries, including MR GRENVILLE'S DIARY OF POLITICAL EVENTS, while First Lord of the Treasury. Edited, with Notes. 4 Vols. 8vo. 64s.
———— (JAMES & HORACE) Rejected Addresses. *Twenty-third Edition.* Fcap. 8vo. 1s., or *Fine Paper,* with Portrait. Fcap. 8vo. 5s.
———— (THOMAS ASSHETON) Reminiscences of his Life **and** Pursuits. By SIR EARDLEY WILMOT. Illustrations. 8vo.

SPECKTER'S (OTTO) Puss in Boots, suited to the Tastes of Old and Young. *A New Edition.* With 12 Woodcuts. Square 12mo. 1s. 6d.
———————— Charmed Roe; or, the Story of the Little Brother and Sister. Illustrated. 16mo.

STANLEY'S (Rev. A. P.) ADDRESSES AND CHARGES OF THE LATE BISHOP STANLEY. With a Memoir of his Life. *Second Edition.* 8vo. 10s. 6d.
———————— Sermons preached in Canterbury Cathedral, on the Unity of Evangelical and Apostolical Teaching. Post 8vo. 7s. 6d.
———————— Commentary on St. Paul's Epistles to the Corinthians, with Notes and Dissertations. *Second, and revised Edition.* 8vo. 18s.
———————— Historical Memorials of Canterbury. The Landing of Augustine—The Murder of Becket—The Black Prince—The Shrine of Becket. *Third Edition.* Woodcuts. Post 8vo. 7s. 6d.
———————— Sinai and Palestine, in Connexion with their History. *Sixth Edition.* Map. 8vo. 16s.

ST. JOHN'S (CHARLES) Wild Sports and Natural History of the Highlands. Post 8vo. 6s.
———————— (BAYLE) Adventures in the Libyan Desert and the Oasis of Jupiter Ammon. Woodcuts. Post 8vo. 2s. 6d.

STEPHENSON'S (GEORGE) Life. The Railway Engineer. By SAMUEL SMILES. *Fifth Edition.* Portrait. 8vo. 16s.
———————— The Story of his Life. By SAMUEL SMILES. *Fifth Thousand.* Woodcuts. Post 8vo. 6s.

STOTHARD'S (THOS., R. A.) Life. With Personal Reminiscences. By Mrs. BRAY. With Portrait and 60 Woodcuts. 4to.

STREET'S (G. E.) Brick and Marble Architecture of Italy, in the Middle Ages. Plates. 8vo. 21s.

STRIFE FOR THE MASTERY. Two Allegories. With Illustrations. Crown 8vo. 6s.

SWIFT'S (JONATHAN) Life, Letters and Journals. By JOHN FORSTER. 8vo. *In Preparation.*
———————— Works. Edited, with Notes. By JOHN FORSTER. 8vo. *In Preparation.*

SYDENHAM'S (LORD) Memoirs. With his Administration in Canada. By G. POULET SCROPE, M.P. *Second Edition.* Portrait. 8vo. 9s. 6d.

SYMES (JAS.) Principles of Surgery. *Fourth Edition.* 8vo. 14s.

TAYLOR'S (HENRY) Notes from Life. Fcap 8vo. 2s.
———————— (J. E.) Fairy Ring. A Collection of Stories for Young Persons. From the German. With Illustrations by RICHARD DOYLE. *Second Edition.* Woodcuts. Fcap. 8vo.

TENNENT'S (SIR J. E.) Christianity in Ceylon. Its Introduction and Progress under the Portuguese, Dutch, British, and American Missions. With an Historical Sketch of the Brahmanical and Buddhist Superstitions. Woodcuts. 8vo. 14s.

THOMSON'S (DR. A. S.) Story of New Zealand; Past and Present —Savage and Civilised. Maps and Illustrations. 2 Vols. Post 8vo. 24s.

THREE-LEAVED MANUAL OF FAMILY PRAYER; arranged so as to save the trouble of turning the Pages backwards and forwards. Royal 8vo. 2s.

TICKNOR'S (GEORGE) History of Spanish Literature. With Criticisms on particular Works, and Biographical Notices of Prominent Writers. *Second Edition.* 3 Vols. 8vo. 24s.

TOCQUEVILLE'S (M. DE) State of France before the Revolution, 1789, and on the Causes of that Event. Translated by HENRY REEVE, Esq. 8vo. 14s.

TREMENHEERE'S (H. S.) Political Experience of the Ancients,
in its bearing on Modern Times. Fcap. 8vo. 2s. 6d.

———————————— Notes on Public Subjects, made during a
Tour in the United States and Canada. Post 8vo. 10s. 6d.

———————————— Constitution of the United States compared
with our own. Post 8vo. **9s. 6d.**

TWISS' (HORACE) Public and Private Life of Lord Chancellor Eldon,
with Selections from his Correspondence. Portrait. *Third Edition.*
2 Vols. Post 8vo. 21s.

TYNDALL'S (JOHN) Glaciers of the Alps. Being a Narrative of
various Excursions among them, and an Account of Three Years'
Observations and Experiments on their Motion, Structure, and General
Phenomena. Post 8vo. *In the Press.*

TYTLER (PATRICK FRASER), A Memoir of. By his Friend, REV.
J. W. BURGON, M.A. *Second Edition.* 8vo. 9s.

UBICINI'S (M. A.) Letters on Turkey and its Inhabitants—the
Moslems, Greeks, Armenians, &c. Translated by LADY EASTHOPE.
2 Vols. Post 8vo. 21s.

VAUGHAN'S (REV. DR.) Sermons preached in Harrow School.
8vo. 10s. 6d.

———————————— New Sermons. **12mo.** 5s.

VENABLES' (REV. R. L.) Domestic Scenes in Russia during a
Year's Residence, chiefly in the Interior. *Second Edition.* Post 8vo. 5s.

VOYAGE to the Mauritius and back, touching at the Cape of Good
Hope, and St. Helena. By Author of "PADDIANA." Post 8vo. 9s. 6d.

WAAGEN'S (DR.) Treasures of Art in Great Britain. Being an
Account of the Chief Collections of Paintings, Sculpture, Manuscripts,
Miniatures, &c. &c., in this Country Obtained from Personal Inspec-
tion during Visits to England. 3 Vols. 8vo. 36s.

———————————— Galleries and Cabinets of Art in England. Being
an Account of more than Forty Collections, visited in 1854-56 and
never before described. With Index. 8vo. 18s.

WADDINGTON'S (DEAN) Condition and Prospects of the
Greek Church. *New Edition.* Fcap. 8vo. 3s. 6d.

WAKEFIELD'S (E. J.) Adventures in New Zealand. With
some Account of the Beginning of the British Colonisation of the
Island. Map. 2 Vols. 8vo. 28s.

WALKS AND TALKS. A Story-book for Young Children. By
AUNT IDA. With Woodcuts. 16mo. 5s.

WARD'S (ROBERT PLUMER) Memoir, Correspondence, Literary and
Unpublished Diaries and Remains. By the HON. EDMUND PHIPPS.
Portrait. 2 Vols. 8vo. 28s.

WATT'S (JAMES) Life. Incorporating the most interesting passages from his Private and Public Correspondence. By JAMES P.
MUIRHEAD, M.A. *Second Edition.* Portraits and Woodcuts. 8vo. 16s.

———————————— Origin and Progress of his Mechanical Inventions. Illustrated by his Correspondence with his Friends. Edited by J. P.
MUIRHEAD. Plates. 3 vols. 8vo. 45s., or Large Paper. 3 Vols. 4to.

WILKIE'S (SIR DAVID) Life, Journals, Tours, and Critical Remarks
on Works of Art, with a Selection from his Correspondence. By ALLAN
CUNNINGHAM. Portrait. 3 Vols. 8vo. 42s.

WOOD'S (LIEUT.) Voyage up the Indus to the Source of the
River Oxus, by Kabul and Badakhshan. Map. 8vo. 14s.

WELLINGTON'S (The Duke of) Despatches during his various Campaigns. Compiled from Official and other Authentic Documents. By Col. Gurwood, C.B. *New Enlarged Edition.* 8 Vols. 8vo. 21s. each.

———————— Supplementary Letters, Despatches, and other Papers relating to India. Edited by his Son. 4 Vols. 8vo. 20s. each.

———————— Civil Correspondence and Memoranda, while Chief Secretary for Ireland, from 1807 to 1809. 8vo. 20s.

———————— Selections from his Despatches and General Orders. By Colonel Gurwood. 8vo. 18s.

———————— Speeches in Parliament. 2 Vols. 8vo. 42s.

WILKINSON'S (Sir J. G.) Popular Account of the Private Life, Manners, and Customs of the Ancient Egyptians. *New Edition.* Revised and Condensed. With 500 Woodcuts. 2 Vols. Post 8vo. 12s.

———————— Dalmatia and Montenegro; with a Journey to Mostar in Hertzegovina, and Remarks on the Slavonic Nations. Plates and Woodcuts. 2 Vols. 8vo. 42s.

———————— Handbook for Egypt.—Thebes, the Nile, Alexandria, Cairo, the Pyramids, Mount Sinai, &c. Map. Post 8vo. 15s.

———————— On Colour, and on the Necessity for a General Diffusion of Taste among all Classes; with Remarks on laying out Dressed or Geometrical Gardens. With Coloured Illustrations and Woodcuts. 8vo. 18s.

———————— (G. B.) Working Man's Handbook to South Australia; with Advice to the Farmer, and Detailed Information for the several Classes of Labourers and Artisans. Map. 18mo. 1s. 6d.

WILSON'S (Rev. D., late Lord Bishop of Calcutta) Life, with Extracts from his Letters and Journals. By Rev. Josiah Bateman, M.A. Portrait and Illustrations. 2 Vols. 8vo. 28s.

———————— (Genl. Sir Robert) Journal, while employed at the Head Quarters of the Russian Army on a special mission during the Invasion of Russia, and Retreat of the French Army, 1812. 8vo.

WORDSWORTH'S (Rev. Dr.) Athens and Attica. Journal of a Tour. *Third Edition.* Plates. Post 8vo. 8s. 6d.

———————— Greece: Pictorial, Descriptive, and Historical, with a History of Greek Art, by G. Scharf, F.S.A. *New Edition.* With 600 Woodcuts. Royal 8vo. 28s.

———————— King Edward VIth's Latin Grammar, for the Use of Schools. *12th Edition*, revised. 12mo. 3s. 6d.

———————— First Latin Book, or the Accidence, Syntax and Prosody, with English Translation for Junior Classes. *Third Edition.* 12mo. 2s.

WORNUM (Ralph). A Biographical Dictionary of Italian Painters: with a Table of the Contemporary Schools of Italy. By a Lady. Post 8vo. 6s. 6d.

———————— Epochs of Painting Characterised; a Sketch of the History of Painting, showing its gradual and various development from the earliest ages to the present time. *New Edition*, Woodcuts. Post 8vo. 6s.

WROTTESLEY'S (Lord) Thoughts on Government and Legislation. Post 8vo. 7s. 6d.

YOUNG'S (Dr. Thos.) Life and Miscellaneous Works, edited by Dean Peacock and John Leitch. Portrait and Plates. 4 Vols. 8vo. 15s. each.

BRADBURY AND EVANS, PRINTERS, WHITEFRIARS.

www.ingramcontent.com/pod-product-compliance
Lightning Source LLC
Chambersburg PA
CBHW021126270326
41929CB00009B/1057